The Little Greige Book
The Art of War for Flooring

This book is about taking people, raw, unpolished, and authentic, and guiding them through the finishing school of experience, insight, data, and growth. Just as greige goods are the essential beginning of all textiles, this book treats each reader as a work in progress, worthy of refinement but valuable from the start. It's for those who are either casting new swords or sharpening older ones.

The inspiration came from Harvey Penick's "Little Red Book", what might be the definitive work on the subject of golf and how to improve your game. His teaching philosophy centered on the belief that each player possesses unique physical characteristics and learning styles, requiring individualized instruction rather than one-size-fits-all solutions.

This book is about sharing experiences in an industry I became passionate about, in the hopes that it will be useful in the quest of competency and understanding.

Dedication

This book is dedicated to all those who helped me live a good life within an industry that became more than just a career, it became a passion.

I found my way to it accidentally and with no understanding at the time that it could bring me a full and meaningful life. I was just looking for a job. One in which I could raise a family, get my kids an education, and retire comfortably. Old school American Dream stuff.

To the mentors who took time they may not have had to give, the leaders who gave me a shot when I hadn't yet earned it, and the colleagues who challenged, sharpened, and believed in me along the way.

Some chapters with each of them closed graciously. Others ended indecorously. But all of them mattered deeply. Thank you.

This book is a small acknowledgement of a large debt owed to those who showed me what this industry could be when done with purpose, grit, and heart.

© 2025 by Peter Rincione. All rights reserved.

No part of this publication may be reproduced, stored in a retrieval system, or transmitted in any form or by any means—electronic, mechanical, photocopying, recording, or otherwise—without prior written permission from the publisher.

Published by: Peter Rincione via IngramSpark

www.ingramspark.com

ISBN: 9798218691295

LCCN: 2025913416

Cover and interior design by Peter Rincione

The cover art, spine layout, and back cover design were conceived and created by the author using a combination of original concept sketching, digital layout tools, and layout specifications required by IngramSpark's publishing platform.

Printed in the United States of America

First Edition

Preface

The Flooring industry is a solid and dependable supplier of happiness and prosperity to its human capital. It also makes incredible imaginative products. This book aims to demonstrate that, along with some data and techniques to help you attain, not only a comprehensive understanding of its drivers, but to help in your confidence in understanding and articulating it as you move through its channels. It's intended as a guideline for those who understand that passion is acquired through mastery.

It's for those in a particular industry, the 330,000 or so who populate the flooring supply chain ecosystem. It works within any supply chain, but this one, for later reasons discussed, happens to reference flooring. The higher up the organization chart you are, the more utility you should derive from it. It'll be like having the Pegasus Boots in The Legend of Zelda.

Some Lessons shown were learned through a personal journey of this American enterprise. These chapters relate to the flooring industry, because that's what put meat on the table for my family. I marinated in it for years, soaking up its flavors like Tofu. It both flavored and nourished me. The disease and its curse as Shakespear might say. This industry can do the same for you. Sustainably.

Yes, it burns oil occasionally, but no worries, greed has almost always saved us from demise. (Wink)

The Lessons within apply universally to all of the subcontract trades really. These are supply chain businesses where you will meet the most serious and competent people in industry leadership. From raw materials to completed projects, where most will enthusiastically share their experiences and understanding. This across the landscape of a fully mature biome. This dynamic may not receive as many likes as a top culture podcaster, but it deserves to. Because network understanding and tradecraft are physical laws of the universe. They're undeniable.

There are virtually no elements of this book that are revelatory. There are instances of orbit shifting and velocity changes that describe serious course corrections over time, bounced by winds of change. For the most part, the evolution of this industry to a serious global powerhouse, have been slow progressions of what patent attorneys refer to as "logical extensions of the current state of the art." Not much revolutionary, but also, dependably clever and resiliently evolutionary.

It's also a semi-anonymous business. Barely recognized. This book could have been titled "Camouflage and Convert." Only 11% of consumers can name more than one brand of flooring. Most of those same consumers can name 7 brands of cereal. As Mathew McConaughey famously said in The Wolf of Wall Street, "It doesn't exist. It never landed. It's not on the elemental chart." Yet here it is, decades later, still creating something useful and desired.

I've included takes on the current flooring industry's business tools. The big blinds of the game. They will eventually become artifacts of history, like most infrastructure of industries have over time. Remember EDI? Probably not. Those I discuss are relevant only now. The narratives include the impacts of AI, quantitative analysis, IoT product integration, blockchain, cloud computing, omnichannel models, and robotics. Relevant, at least for today.

Flooring is one of many trades stitched to construction, a $14T global business backstop. It's a nearly perfect example of the cycle of commerce in America from the imaginings of 20th century entrepreneurship to private equity and meta-data harvesters enthusiastically intruding today. From birth to maturity, with common elements of success and failure noted along the way.

Yes, In the spectrum of interesting things, floorings in the red zone of buzzkill. I mean, has anyone, ever, said "Let's go check out Carpet Exchange next Friday night"? Seriously? Imagine going to a party and have someone come up and introduce themselves as being in the flooring industry. I'd think, 'Why me? It's my only night out this month?"

It's not SpaceX sexy, true. But it's an industry that quietly built thousands of millionaires. A gritty durable American enterprise for success. Along the way I hope you'll see its potential to color and enhance your own prosperity and happiness. To help make you serious about your role. To move you from greige to finished.

My hope is to showcase this mature American industry as an example of why anyone driven to entrepreneurship should consider it an ideal place to grab a rung on the ladder of U.S commerce at its most inventive and durable.

Table of Contents

Chapter 1: Welcome to Broadloomistan... 1
The Flooring World Tries to Keep Up

    Land of the Looped and Tufted 2

    Founders Without Headshots 3

    Rivals to the Throne.............................5

    Global Interlopers 6

    Why It Still Rules 7

Chapter 2: History Underfoot...................11
How Americas Flooring Industry
Continually Disrupts Itself

    1950s: The Original Platform Play 12

    1960s: Scaling the Unscalable 13

    1970s: Crisis Drives Innovation..........14

    1980s: Consolidation and Branding...14

    1990s: The Platform Shift....................15

    2000s: Global Gain/Recession Pain ..16

    2010s: LVT Breaks Everything........... 17

    2020s: The AI Powered Floor..............18

    Economic Forecasting 18

    Winners and Losers 19

Chapter 3: Dark Knights Among Us 23
PE's Role in the Flooring Industry

    Equity's Private Hunting Ground...... 24

    Why the Interest? 26

Healthy Margins & Cash Flow 28
Consolidation and Pricing Power 29
Stability with Upside 30
PE's Effect Across the Supply Chain . 32
Manufacturers: Strategic Roulette 32
Risks of Musical Chair Ownership. ... 33
Distributors: Vying for Relevance: 34
Retail Moves: 37
Installers and Service Providers: 40
Surf the Private Equity Wave 44
Preparing for a PE Deal 57
Find Your Footing in a PE Future 63

Chapter 4: Zero Sum Nightmare 69
Low Growth Trench Warfare

The Great Compression 70
The Independents' Dilemma 71
The Path to Survival 72
Situational Awareness 73

Chapter 5: Do Brands Still Matter? 77
Only When It's Your Own

The Reckoning 78
4 Singularities of Brand Building 79
The Innovation Imperative 82
The Differentiation Paradox 83
From Commodity to Community 83

Chapter 6 - Hidden Earthquakes 87
When Surfaces Start Shifting

    The Rise of SIN 88

    Surfaces as Data Infrastructure......... 89

    The Materials Arms Race.................... 89

    AI Is Not Coming for Flooring........... 90

    The Great De-synchronization 91

Chapter 7: Don't be a Blackberry 93
Without Reinvention, Legacy Dies

    Disruption Doesn't Ask Permission. . 94

    Life-or-Death Metrics 94

    3 Deadly Sins....................... 995

    Survival Playbook 96

    The Bottom Line 98

    Winds of Change................................. 98

Chapter 8: Texas Roadhouse Yourself .. 101
How Tech Keeps You on the Menu

    Texas Two-Step....................102

    Quick Stats 102

    Flooring Clustercuss 102

    The Reckoning 103

    Solution: Digital Floor Operations ...103

    Key Component Criteria: 104

    The Money Shot 104

    4 Singularities 105

Winners and Losers 106

Truth Bomb 107

The Path Forward 107

Chapter 9: Let's Keiretsu 109
What the Japanese Supply Chain Model Can Teach Us

The Godfather of Supply Chains 111

Swipe Left on Stability 111

Moment of Truth 112

Should Flooring Go Full Keiretsu? ... 113

Is Loyalty the New Margin? 114

Chapter 10: The AI Imperative 117
Without AI, You're the New Blocbuster

The Problem 119

A Solution 120

Imperative Non-Negotiables 121

What's it all about, Alpha? 122

Byproduct Halo Effects 123

AI is Essential 121

Hard Truth 124

AI Future—Plan or Be Planned 125

Chapter 11: Inflation Arbitrage 129
How Floor Purchases Reveal a Hidden Price Psychology

Numbers Don't Lie 130

  Psychological Arbitrage 131

  Memory Pricing Beats CPI 131

  Quality Trumps Price........................ 131

  Reframe the Conversation 132

  Value Stacking 132

  Winners: 132

  Losers: 133

  Bottom Line 133

Chapter 12: Latency 135
Industries Silent Killer

  The New Currency: Speed 137

  Flooring Journey Triage: 138

  5 Hacks to Flooring at Speed 138

Chapter 13: Leadership 143
The Energy that Fuels the Enterprise.

  4 Horsemen of Flooring Leadership 144

  Confidence Is Your Underlayment ... 144

  Vision + Execution = Unstoppable ... 145

  Your Energy Management is Key 146

  Assert With Strategic Patience 147

  The Reckoning 147

  Leaderships Bottom Line 148

Chapter 14: Board Stiff 151
The Missed Opportunity of Governance.

  What Should Your Board Do? 152

    What Should Your Board Ask? 153

    What Actually Happens 153

    Boardroom as Waroom 154

Chapter 15: Dead Zones of Demand 157
Spotting Potholes in Your Market.

    Drucker's Opportunistic Corridors ... 158

    Data to Ruin Your Morning Coffee: . 159

    4 Horsemen of Retail Death 159

    4 Dimensions of Manifestation: 160

    4 Escape Routes 161

    The Great Bifurcation 163

Chapter 16: The Quantum Floor 167
Where Uncertainty Meets Installation

    Explore the Flooring Cosmos. 168

    The Observer Effect 169

    You Can't Know Everything at Once 170

    Quantum Tunneling 171

    Wave-Particle Duality 171

    Schrodingers Floor 172

    The Quantum Observatory 172

Chapter 17: The Margin Paradox 175
Why Only 10% of New Businesses Become Legacies

    Flooring Economics 176

    The Revenue Reality 177

Industry Context 178
The Margin Trap 178
The Startup Cash Burn 179
The Failure Reality 180
Paths Forward 181
The Take 183
4 Horsemen Pillars for Success 184
Digitize Your Enterprise 185
Mobilize 186
Verticalize 187
Monetize 188

Chapter 18: Buying Groups 193
The Velvet Handshake

GPOs are Force Multipliers 194
4 Roles of a GPO 195
GPOs Quietly Shaping Markets 196
Time to Let Go the Handshake 197
Any Shame in it? 197

Chapter 19: The Gritty Bunch 201
The Tribe that Builds Us

More than Muscle Memory 202
We're Tribal, Not Local 204
Signal Through the Noise 205
No Glamor, All Guts 206
Surface Tension 207

Conclusion: The Floor Is Yours 209
Bibliography ii
Books ii
Articles and Web Sources............................ iii
Quotations from Public Figures...................vi
Write Some Notes viii

Chapter 1: Welcome to Broadloomistan

The Flooring World Tries to Keep Up

Industries don't flourish by accident. Well, maybe podcasting. They metastasize when something elemental shifts. When a product doesn't just enter the market but reshapes it. Broadloom carpet wasn't merely a new way to cover floors; it was a seminal shift in how Americans thought about space, comfort, and efficiency.

What made it flourish wasn't just tufting machines or cheap synthetic fiber. It was ubiquity by design. Carpet became the default because it was fast, forgiving, and could roll over complexity with ease. It bypassed the artisanal, undercut the expensive, and made interiors soft, uniform, and scalable.

"The competitor to be feared is one who never bothers about you at all but goes on making his own business better all the time."

— Henry Ford

Tucked into the rolling foothills of Northwest Georgia, just past the Waffle House that time forgot, sits a place that built the modern American floor. You won't find it in Fast Company or Wired. You won't hear tech bros or coastal strategists expound on it at TED. But if you've ever walked down a hotel corridor, paced a classroom in sock feet, bounced a ball in a gym, or rolled your luggage through an airport without realizing the flooring finish has a name, you've brushed up against the empire.

Let's call it Broadloomistan.

Not technically, of course. The postal address is Dalton, Georgia. But that's like calling Las Vegas Clark County. Dalton is a location. Broadloomistan is an ecosystem, a mythos. A flooring mecca. A 40-mile stretch of compressed capitalism along I-75 where yarn, ambition, polyester, and a near-religious commitment to volume come together to create square footage on an epochal scale.

Land of the Looped and Tufted

Broadloomistan isn't flashy. Its idea of a startup is a third-generation yarn converter with a new compounding line. But don't confuse grit for lack of sophistication. This town put more R&D into primary backing and thermal fusion than most sectors put into AI.

You like innovation? Broadloomistan's been innovating since before you could pronounce polypropylene. It invented the mass production of tufted carpet. It engineered continuous dye ranges the length of football fields. It figured out how to recycle Coke bottles into fiber, before it was cool, and then quietly scaled that to millions of square yards without bothering to write a press release.

Where Silicon Valley disrupts, Broadloomistan delivers. Where tech loves a pitch deck, Northwest Georgia loves a forklift with a carpet pole.

Founders Without Headshots

This region doesn't do glossy bios or vision boards. Its hall of fame is paved with pragmatists:

Bob Shaw, the industrialist-king. He didn't just scale Shaw Industries, he built a vertically integrated machine that turned Dalton into something just short of a sovereign state. There is no one I've talked to across the globe in my consulting practice that is unfamiliar with Shaw industries. Making a flooring brand recognizable is an incredible feat.

M.B. "Bud" Seretean, who made Coronet a force, then retired into motivational speaking. Because honestly, once you've dealt with distribution reps in 1980s

Mississippi, you can teach resilience to anyone.

Colman Kahn, an EQ visionary who saw the power of a specific niche business model focused exclusively on commercial flooring finishes. And then bundled that together in a cultural model that made family a primary consideration in how they operated. In the market that he operated in he midwifed its current most prolific players. He saw them all develop maintenance businesses as an adjunct, keeping a touch point with his end users. His original business, Kahn and Company, was the prototype for what we see currently. Giants like Diverzify operate with his DNA strand. See, sometimes boomers have been useful.

Waldo Semon, a chemist working for B F Goodrich in the 1920's who, seeking a substitute for the flexibility of rubber, created the first plasticized version of PVC, the precursor to modern vinyl flooring.

And the Tufting Machine Whisperers, unnamed, unphotographed, but responsible for the breakthroughs that let Dalton dominate color, pattern, and price per square yard in a single shift.

These aren't founders in the TED Talk sense. They're builders in the literal sense. They wear work boots, understand the Pythagorean theorem and carry digital measuring devices. And when they invent something, it shows up in your warehouse next week, not in a pitch deck three funding rounds from now. There are no statutes of them anywhere, but they're visible every time you step into a room.

Rivals to the Throne

Naturally, other American towns have tried to claw away some of Broadloomistan's turf.

Calhoun, GA turned itself into a kind of vinyl Vatican, churning out rigid core as fast as the trucks can be loaded. But Calhoun is still just Dalton's loud little brother with a factory direct website and a chipboard problem.

Edison, NJ tried to style itself the design and spec capital of the Northeast. But after a few rounds of bankruptcy bingo and some gently expired adhesive, it settled into retirement as the place where flooring goes to get rebranded.

Lancaster, PA, with its Armstrong pedigree, could've been flooring's Camelot. Now it mostly serves as a museum for better days, but with a side hustle in LVT imports and nostalgic sales decks. AHF is giving it a makeover, but it's still feels like Sunset Boulevard.

Even Cartersville, GA got fancy with tile and tried to differentiate itself on "design," but you can't unseat Broadloomistan with glazes and grout lines. Not when Dalton's shipping volume would bury your whole portfolio by next Tuesday.

Global Interlopers

Then came the internationals. And this time, they weren't playing.

China built a whole new map. Cities like Changzhou, Haining, and Zhangjiagang became global flooring factories overnight. This was the foreshadowing of how being the lowest cost producers can capture an industry. Not content to just white label for U.S. brands, companies like Novalis, Tajima, and Dajulong invested in German lines, European design teams, and entire PVC supply chains. You can practically smell the extrusion lines from orbit.

They don't just make product, they launch brands. And in the race to undercut mid-market residential vinyl, they're not barbarians at the gate, they're already inside examining your area rugs.

South Korea brought its own playbook: clean specs, high-performance commercial vinyl, and actual R&D budgets. LG Hausys and Hanwha aren't here for your living room. That will be later. Right now they want your hospital wings, labs, and tech campuses.

India, with players like Responsive Industries, is going after volume the old-fashioned way. Commodity LVT at global scale, shipped out of massive ports and into cost-sensitive projects where spec is a suggestion and margin is everything.

Europe, meanwhile, continues the long game. Forbo, Gerflor, and Tarkett lean on legacy, green credentials, and architectural cachet. They don't compete on price. They compete on conscience.

And still, Broadloomistan holds.

Why It Still Rules

Because it's not just about having mills. It's about having a mill town. An ecosystem. A shared language spoken in denier, twist level, and the precise angle of a broken feed roller. It's family. It's about being able to call your extrusion guy, your dye chemist, your logistics broker, your college graduate children now working for an end-user, and your cousin the forklift mechanic. All in the same lunch break.

You can copy the product. You can even lease the machinery. But you can't duplicate a 70-year operating system built on institutional knowledge, grudging mutual respect, and the quiet confidence of people who've been running 24-hour shifts since your VP of Innovation was in high school.

Broadloomistan doesn't care about your TikTok campaign or your D2C disruptor branding. It cares about square footage. Ship dates. Needle gauge. And getting the truck out of the bay by 4:45 so the next load can roll just in time.

It doesn't scream. It hums

Chapter 2: History Underfoot

How Americas Flooring Industry Disrupts Itself

The flooring industry is a near perfect case study of American capitalism. This chapter is a macro view of the flooring industries relentless cycle of innovation, disruption, and reinvention and the effects.

"Dance. Even if you have nowhere to do it but the living room floor."

Kurt Vonnegut

The numbers are impressive. The US flooring market hit $32B in 2024. Mordor research forecasts the US market at $62.42B by 2030, with global revenue at $409B in the same period. That's roughly the GDP of Estonia according to the World Bank. Use this to do the math on where you are. If your share starts with a handle on the left side of the percentage, you're killing it. All for the privilege of not walking directly on your subflooring. Life, liberty, and the pursuit of floor coverings.

1950s: The Original Platform Play

Post-WWII, America needed houses. Millions of them. And these houses needed floors. Fast and cheap.

Enter the tufting machine, a Southern states innovation that did to woven carpets what Walmart would later do to Main Street retail. By the end of the decade, traditional carpet makers were toast.

This wasn't evolution; it was extinction. Nylon (Thank you war science) gave these carpets durability at a fraction of the cost. The American middle class responded by covering every square inch of their homes in wall-to-wall synthetic carpet. Hardwood's market share collapsed from 22% to 2%. That's two percent!

That's not disruption; that's an industry mass casualty event.

Meanwhile, vinyl flooring staged its own coup against linoleum. Armstrong and Mannington introduced vinyl that promised the mid-century dream: a future where housewives (quaint) never had to wax floors again.

(Don't blame me, that's how it was marketed.) The consumer demanded convenience, and the market delivered. Spoiler: this pattern repeats.

1960s: Scaling the Unscalable

The 1960s were flooring boom years. American carpet production tripled in a decade. That's 3X. Tufted carpet reached 85% market share, delivering catastrophic returns for legacy woven carpet manufacturers and other disbelievers.

Classic disruption side effect: the product was objectively worse in some ways (durability, longevity) but 10x better on convenience, price, coolness.

Vinyl continued its march, introducing cushioned backing and genuinely no-wax finishes. The consumer proposition was irresistible: floors that look good with zero maintenance. How do you compete with zero?

Hardwood continued circling the drain, relegated to history like steam engines and phone booths. Or so we thought.

1970s: Crisis Drives Innovation

Oil embargoes. Stagflation. Recession. The 1970s were brutal, and housing took a face plant. Half of all carpet mills shuttered or scaled back by the early '80s.

The survivors weren't necessarily the biggest but the most adaptable. They vertically integrated, controlling everything from raw materials to installation, and improved delivery.

The Lesson? When your industry faces an existential threat, incremental late change is stakeholder nightmare fuel.

Even amid this chaos, innovation accelerated. Stain-resistant carpets emerged (Scotchgard protection being the iPhone of carpet treatments), and the first wood-look vinyl planks appeared, the Godparent of today's LVT phenomenon.

Innovation didn't pause during downturns; it accelerated.

1980s: Consolidation and Branding

The '80s were when scale became the unassailable advantage. The flooring equivalent of "nobody ever got fired for buying IBM" was "nobody ever got fired for buying Stainmaster." In 1986, DuPont dropped $26 million on Stainmaster advertising, making carpet fiber a conversation topic at dinner parties. That is a genuinely insane achievement.

By the '90s, four companies controlled 80% of all carpet production in America. Mohawk alone devoured a dozen competitors. Since 1990 they have acquired a total of 34 companies.

Warren Buffett saw the writing on the wall. Berkshire Hathaway acquired Shaw Industries. When Berkshire buys an industry leader, you're doing something right.

The era of the family-owned carpet mill was over. Scale won. Distribution won. Brand won.

1990s: The Platform Shift

The '90s economy roared, and consumers suddenly wanted hardwood floors again. The industry had left hardwood for dead, and it came roaring back like a zombie with good taste.

Factory-finished engineered wood made installation faster and cheaper, addressing hardwood's traditional pain points. It promised better durability and flawless factory finish over job site finished floors.

Floor prep, bonding technologies, and installation engineering improved characteristics that put speed, safety, process, and environmental concerns on the map.

Then laminate flooring arrived from Europe and changed everything. Pergo's click-together installation (a 1996 innovation) meant homeowners could install floors themselves over a weekend. DIY flooring nation was forged.

This wasn't just a product shift; it was a platform shift. Carpet was iOS, and hard surface was Android. Totally different ecosystems with unique economics, distribution, and consumer expectations.

The Lesson: No market leadership is permanent. Manufacturers who didn't diversify got eaten.

2000s: Global Gain/Recession Pain

The early 2000s housing boom was another flooring gold rush. (Notice the industry's business cycle here?) Then 2008 happened. The crash was an extinction-level event, with giants like Beaulieu filing for bankruptcy in 2017 and Armstrong's flooring division followed suit in 2022. PE begins smelling opportunity.

But the real story was globalization. Chinese-made ceramic tiles, resilient flooring, and laminates flooded the market. Home Depot and Lowe's seized market share from specialty retailers through brute force fueled by massive production capacity. Supply chains stretched across continents. Consumer education and feature awareness blossomed, changing purchase criteria.

The flooring industry experienced what every industry eventually faces: commoditization and disintermediation.

The survivors pivoted to sustainability. LEED certification was born. Recycled fiber, low-VOC adhesives, environmental considerations evolved. When you can't win on price, you differentiate or die.

2010s: LVT Breaks Everything

Luxury vinyl tile and plank (LVT) did to flooring what Netflix did to Blockbuster. The category exploded from 12% market share in 2014 to 24% by 2019, doubling in five years. CEOs became concerned that this category would cannibalize all of its other product offering. At this writing it continues to usurp share logarithmically from all other finish categories. Although at this writing there are finally signs of equilibrium showing?

Why? LVT solved the consumer's impossible triangle: beautiful aesthetics, bulletproof durability, and affordable prices. That's a Pick 3. Something previously impossible in flooring.

The giants raced to acquire LVT specialists or build capacity. Traditional retailers scrambled to adapt as augmented reality apps let consumers preview floors in their homes. The digital transformation had arrived in one of America's former most analog industries.

2020s: The AI Powered Floor

Today, we're watching the early stages of flooring's next reinvention.

AI-monitored production lines spot defects in real-time. Smart supply chains use predictive analytics to optimize inventory. Blockchain is emerging. One-of-a-kind floors can be designed online and manufactured on-demand. AI Implementation into retail is creating augmented super closers. IoT flooring integration is awakening, offering health monitoring as a feature.

Economic Forecasting

Someone said economic forecasting only exists to make astrology seem credible, but here goes.

Within a decade, floors will be technology platforms. We'll see embedded sensors turning your living spaces into an IoT-connected surface. Your floor will monitor your gait to detect early signs of Parkinson's. It will measure steps and usage patterns in public spaces. It will adjust temperature automatically based on occupancy patterns. It will lead in biomimicry, copying the efficient physics and designs inherent in nature.

The next disruption isn't just a new material; it's the convergence of flooring with computing. The floor becomes the platform.

DTC variants, like BuildDirect, will continue the compression of both distributors and retailers.

Robots will be installing the bulk of flooring finishes and doing the surface prep.

Amazon will buy the industry.

Winners and Losers

The biggest Lesson from 70 years of flooring history? Winning is temporary.

The mills that dominated the carpet boom of the '60s are down to a handful or have become portfolio companies, abdicating their former empire building cultures to ROI. The laminate pioneers of the '90s lost to LVT in the 2010s.

Each generation of flooring leaders eventually faced their Kodak/Blackberry moment, clinging to outdated business models while upstarts rewrote the rules.

The survivors had three common trace elements:

1. They embraced technological disruption early and often

2. They vertically integrated to mitigate destiny

3. They recognized that consumer preferences are the only north star that matters

This isn't just about floors. It's about how industries evolve, how disruption works, and how capitalism's creative destruction never takes a day off when it senses consumer desire.

Chapter 3: Dark Knights Among Us

Private Equity's Role in Flooring

This chapter comes in early as it describes the mechanics and metrics of what private equity uses to invest and assign value to their interests. In other words, a good overview of the current state of the union in flooring in best practices, values, and key performance indicators (KPI). Private equity's role in the flooring industry is the acid test on the dynamics that drive and sustain it.

"The greatest fortunes are built when the world goes through massive change."

Dan Sullivan

Flash forward to 2025. This chapter comes early as it is a 40,000-foot view of the current state of the industry. As a stand-alone subject it's important. But this chapter also provides an overview and foundation for later ones. Much like a SWOT exercise in how we play.

Equity's Private Hunting Ground

The flooring industry isn't just planks, tiles, and carpet rolls, it's a big business.

In the U.S. alone, floor covering sales at manufacturer sell were about $34.1 billion in 2024. $134 billion with all channel partner margins and labor. Globally, flooring is a massive market valued around $311 billion globally in 2024. Capital is taking notice. In recent years, private equity firms flooded into every channel of this sector. Capital is flowing into flooring like no time in its history, Equity is snapping up privately held businesses and regional chains with the voracity of a shopaholic at a Shein sale.

Why the frenzy? What else, opportunity. The flooring business is highly fragmented. Roughly 85% of flooring retailers are single-store operations. New entrants fail at a 90% rate. Only 10 to 15% of all flooring suppliers are legacy after a 70-year run. In other words, it's a giant industry with no single behemoth in charge. For private equity

(PE), that's like an aphrodisiac. Fragmentation means hundreds of small players ripe for consolidation, and PE investors see a chance to roll up these independents into formidable national platforms. They're essentially betting they can turn a patchwork main street shop into the next Home Depot or Floor & Decor.

Upticks in financial metrics, a success story in a mature industry like flooring, has created an accelerant for interest. The average gross and net margins of high performers improved from the low to mid-single digit percentages, to the low double-digits over the past decade.

And speaking of Floor & Decor (FND): this hard-surface retail upstart was acquired by Ares Management and Freeman Spogli in 2010 (Inc.'s Founder-Friendly Investors list 2021–2024, and under their stewardship, grew into a nationwide powerhouse that went public in 2017. Market cap $7.8B at this writing. That's the kind of success story that makes investors pop bottles of Cristal. That success ginned up even more PE interest in our industry. Like flies to honey.

Private equity's footprint today spans the full flooring supply chain. Dozens of manufacturers, distributors, retail, and installation companies now have PE firms as their owners or partners. I've heard some of them are nice.

In the manufacturing segment, storied names have changed hands. Armstrong Flooring's assets were busted up in bankruptcy and sold to AHF Products (backed by Paceline Equity Partners) in 2022. In 2023, in a move of bold resilience, AHF acquired Crossville Inc. (a major tile producer) to broaden its portfolio.

Distributors have seen similar action. In late 2023, Los Angeles-based Transom Capital acquired Galleher, LLC, the third-largest flooring distributor in the U.S. (Way to go Jeff), from a previous PE owner. I've always asked, "why sell flooring when you can arbitrage, right?"

And on the retail side, specialty flooring chains, in their various species, are being rolled up at a remarkable pace. I'll dive into those examples soon. The bottom line is that private equity now owns a significant slice of what we, the 300,000 professionals in this industry, do every day. The barbarians aren't at the gate, they're already in the living room, examining the rugs.

Why the Interest?

The flooring sector is a textbook example of a disparate market with mature industry levels of standardization. No single company controls a dominant share. There's actually two of them, but that's another later story.

Instead, tens of thousands of independent businesses collectively service end-users.

Flooring retail is 75% composed of one-store businesses with no alpha. That's Latin for target rich PE environment. By acquiring and merging multiple small firms, private equity aims to create the magic fairy dust of economies of scale. Bulk purchasing deals with suppliers, disintermediation, shared warehousing, unified tech stacks, and synergy value. All built out of small local pieces.

We've watched this play out with organizations like Artisan Design Group (ADG), which was formed in 2016 by combining two contractors.

When PE firm The Sterling Group acquired ADG in 2018, the acquisition machine jumped to light speed. ADG completed 20 acquisitions by the end of 2021. Those acquired companies, ranging from retail storefront chains to commercial contractors, together generated an estimated $1.4 billion in sales. They recently sold to Lowes for $1.325B. That is, Microsoft buys Activision news on CNBC. But it was flooring, so barely a mention outside industry portals. In a fragmented market, merging many into one (A later chapter) unlocks a colossal business that simply didn't exist before in its segment. The ancillary effect is that it also creates Amazon bite sized pieces for a snack later.

Healthy Margins & Cash Flow

Flooring might not be software or biotech, but it has what most investors cherish: solid cash flows. When done right, and it can be, flooring businesses can throw off dependable profits and cash flow year after year. Gross margins on flooring products are healthy (often higher than many general retail categories).

Additionally, the infrequency of purchases by flooring end markets creates a hedge against inflation. I address that later in Chapter 12 as that infrequency is a perfect example of the "Corridors of Indifference" theory regarding purchase psychology.

Importantly, flooring sales are tied to the $14 trillion-dollar global construction backstop. The residential and commercial segments, and their various end-user subsets are stable economic engines.

Every time a home is built or sold, or a lease turns over, or Jeff Bezos builds another secure sanctuary on a private island somewhere (Do I sound jealous?), chances are there's a flooring project. That means a recurring revenue stream not easily disrupted by digitizing.

In fact, flooring retail has proven relatively Amazon-proof. So far. Consumers aren't rushing to buy hardwood sight-unseen from a website and install it themselves. They prefer the tactile components of that purchase, seeing materials in person, and relying on expert warranted installation.

Floor & Decor benefited greatly from this dynamic. It grew rapidly without the existential threat e-commerce poses to analog retailers. For private equity, stable demand plus decent stable margins plus limited online disruption equals an attractive, "boring" business that can generate steady returns. In Wall Street parlance, a value play.

They like boring if boring makes money.

Consolidation and Pricing Power

By uniting a once-splintered industry, PE backed platforms can gain pricing power and market clout.

A chain of 30 flooring stores obviously negotiates better deals with suppliers than a lone dealer buying by the pallet. A distributor operating in 10 states can justify investing in state-of-the-art logistics software, data analytics, and multiple mechanized distribution centers, cutting delivery times and costs. Those are moats.

The story PE firm's pitch is that a bigger entity can be more efficient and more competitive, boosting profits in the process. Not quantum computing science, but still fundamental as the North star.

There's also the lure of the "exit multiplier", the idea that a large company will command a higher valuation multiple than several small ones. In other words, five $20 million businesses might each sell at, say, 5x earnings, but a single $100 million platform might fetch 8 or 10X. This multiple expansion through consolidation is PE 101, and flooring's landscape offers prepared soil for it.

Stability with Upside

The flooring sector sits at the crossroads of stability and cyclicality. Day-to-day, it's stable. People always need floors, and much of the business is replacement and renovation.

Which, although still discretionary spending, can't be postponed indefinitely, like congress doing something of value. Floors wear out, styles change. Good I say. Flooring is like a good dividend paying CEF (Closed End Fund). It provides a steady income stream with potential for equity growth.

Consumers purchase flooring 3 to 5 times in their life. That's not many chances at their money. Over the long term, there's cyclicality tied to housing booms and busts, but the breadth of the flooring end markets has a portfolio smoothing effect on the financial and economic traits valued by private equity.

Coming out of the 2020-2021 housing boom, some PE firms pumped money in, noticing a runway of growth. Even though 2023 saw a dip in flooring sales due to high interest rates and a housing cooldown, the commercial side stayed strong.

Multifamily construction was a bright spot. After a sluggish start to 2023 (blame inflation and expensive debt), a surge of deals hit in late 2023. The industry and investors took that as a signal that confidence for 2024 was improving. Rectal forecasting?

Most private equity firms are long in their investment strategy. Typical cycle is to get in, streamline operations, replace entrenched culture (Today that means boomers. Sorry.), expand market share, and exit in 5-7 years with beefed up terminal value. Note the purchase of ADG by Lowes as an example.

The industry has produced a reliable 4.2% CAGR over its history. If you measure its revenue sine wave over history, it's shallow, not many standard deviations away from the mean. That is a measurable sign of relative consistency.

PE's Effect on the Supply Chain

Injecting private equity into a business can feel like jumping on an inclined treadmill. The impact isn't uniform and hits each link of the flooring supply chain a little differently. Let's break it down:

Manufacturers: Strategic Roulette

Flooring manufacturers have seen both opportunity and upheaval with PE involvement. On the plus side, influxes of capital have funded expansion into new product lines and geographies.

A recent example is CFL Flooring (Creative Flooring Solutions), a fast-growing maker of LVT (luxury vinyl) and other materials. In 2021, after growing 50% that year, CFL's founders brought in outside PE investors while keeping majority control. This was specifically to "accelerate international expansion".

The new capital helped CFL ramp up production (they opened a massive new facility in Hunan, China. and invested over $140 million in 18 months, just on growth forecasts. Those damn forecasts again.

Quantum mechanics (More on that in Chapter 13) made that bad timing. It'll be fine, right? It happens. For manufacturers like CFL, private equity money can mean newest factory gear, robotized plant, R&D budget for what's cool, and entrée into new markets that were previously out of reach. Hard ball.

Of course there is a flip side. PE ownership mostly comes with aggressive profit targets and cost-cutting mandates. Shocking. Research revealed that only 36% of the time is a target company's culture a weighted element in the decision-making calculus.

Unstable supply chain dynamics, for any reason, is a stressor for manufacturing operations. It can wreck office cultures. R&D budgets are a target rich environment for cutting to meet short-term earnings goals. All of this potentially sacrifices long-term innovation.

And right now, compute (data processing) leveraged by vision is the primary differentiator. Plus, it's pricey in the scheme of things. Study Tesla.

Risks of Musical Chair Ownership.

A company might get sold from one PE fund to another every few years, causing whiplash in strategy. I trust PE to consider the EQ of that. Not.

A cautionary tale in manufacturing was about a company that created early wealth in an industry. A 150-year-old brand that struggled after being spun off and ultimately went bankrupt in 2022. Its assets ended up with a PE-backed competitor, which was intended to produce, among other things, a legacy second life. But with a possibility of layoffs and plant closures. That's the green mile of company culture.

Lesson: while private equity can inject much-needed capital and modern business practices, it can also come with a dedicated focus on efficiency as the law of the jungle.

For manufacturers, that might mean outsourcing production (good luck), losing employees that cared and understood their role in the CX, squeezing suppliers, hastily churning less profitable product lines.

These and other moves backfire if they alienate customer sets or erode quality.

Distributors: Vying for Relevance:

Flooring distribution, those unsung heroes that get products from mill to market, has been a hotbed of PE activity. It's a double-edged sword. On one hand, being part of a private equity portfolio can supercharge a distributor's growth.

Consider Galleher one of the largest hardwoods and LVT distributors in America. Galleher was acquired by Transom Capital in 2023 with the explicit aim of leveraging PE's resources to "propel the company's growth" and "expand its market reach." That sounds like an AI generated response when asked how they plan to crush it. But nevertheless, they did crush that one.

It means a distributor that was once regional can suddenly think national: opening new branches, acquiring smaller rivals in other regions, beefing up inventory to serve big retail chains, and investing in game changing e-commerce platforms for their dealers.

Private equity can also bring operational expertise, improving routing logistics, optimizing inventory turnover, implementing professional ERP systems, and using the IP of other acquired companies to foment best practices. All the un-sexy stuff that boosts efficiency and profits.

But distributors also face risks when dancing with money men. Distribution is a margin-thin business reliant on relationships. Flooring stores and contractors often stick with distributors who know their business, offer favorable credit terms, and provide reliable service. A new PE owner might push for margin improvement by raising prices or cutting those "extra" services.

They might also pile on debt to finance the acquisition. That's debt that the distribution corpus itself must repay. If a recession hits or sales slow, a heavily leveraged distributor can quickly tip into distress. Believe me, I operated in that exact environment. Very painful.

We've witnessed scenarios where excessive debt and integration hiccups led to service failures, late deliveries, stockouts, driving formerly loyal customers and legacy employees into competitors' arms.

It's astonishing how quickly your annuity class relationships evaporate if you screw up their delivery.

Demise of the Flooring Distribution Group (FDG). is another cautionary tale (The company, part of FDG, defaulted on a loan from ACF Finco I LP, and shuttered what was once a dominant regional hardwood distributor.

Another concern: cultural erosion. A family-owned distributor might have prided itself on personal relationships (the rep who's been calling on a retailer for 20 years, etc.). Post-PE, if that rep is replaced with a call center to cut costs, the goodwill can again evaporate overnight.

Private equity's impact on distribution is a high-wire act. The best cases see smarter, stronger distributors. The worst cases see local goodwill sacrificed on the altar of EBITDA.

Retail Moves:

Perhaps nowhere is PE's presence more visible to the public than in flooring retail. If you needed new carpet or hardwood in the past 5 years, you likely visited a locally owned store.

That's changing. Private equity is busy reassembling regional and national retail flooring chains, and it's shaking up how retailers operate.

A great illustration is the rise of Artisan Design Group (ADG) and others like it. ADG, backed by The Sterling Group, amassed two dozen retail and contractor businesses across the country, totaling roughly $1.4 billion in sales by 2021 Meanwhile, a newer entrant, 31st Street Capital, started around 2019 and has been buying up flooring retailers in major metros, from a 3-store operation in Arizona to an 11-store chain in Minnesota. This often allows retiring owners to "sail into the sunset" while keeping the local brand name intact.

Lowes just purchased ADG for $1.325 billion. So, it goes.

The strategy is clear: grab the market leaders in various cities (usually stores doing $10+ million in sales with strong management, inject professional marketing and operations, and build a powerhouse portfolio of stores that collectively have national scale, if not a national brand (yet).

That is setting the table for Amazon's Sunday roast.

For flooring retailers, PE involvement can bring a lot of positives. Under the hood, many independent flooring dealers are inefficient by modern retail standards. More on that later. They have limited e-commerce presence, minimal data analytics, and often old-school marketing, relying on word-of-mouth and some print ads.

A private equity-backed chain can deploy advanced digital marketing (SEO, social media, targeted ads, AI oversight) and even implement things like in-home shopping technology or centralized call centers to boost sales appointments. That's a relished synergy value.

Moreover, large retail groups negotiate exclusive products or better pricing from manufacturers, meaning better margins and unique offerings. That's the unlimited fuel they show up with to fight their competitors.

Yet not all is rosy on the showroom floor. The risks for retailers under PE can include loss of local touch and autonomy, pressures for high growth at the expense of service, and the perennial specter of over-expansion.

Flooring is still a local service business in many ways. Its installation crews, local builder relationships, community reputation are the exclusivity that this model brings. Pricey but valued with today's consumer.

If a PE-owned retailer imposes one-size-fits-all policies, it might stifle the local savvy that made those stores successful in the first place. I've seen instances where centralizing purchasing led to the wrong product mix for a local market. (Data analytics, discussed later, will help.)

Also, some PE-led retailers accumulate debt and then hit a wall if sales soften. LL Flooring (formerly Lumber Liquidators) is a warning. Though not originally acquired by PE, it struggled in recent years and ended up in Chapter 11 in 2024, ultimately being sold to a private investment firm (F9 Investments) in a bankruptcy fire sale.

LL's story underscores the retail risk, if strategy or market conditions falter, new owners may not have the patience of a family proprietor; they'll cut losses, close stores (LL closed nearly 100 before the sale), or flip the business quickly.

In short, private equity can professionalize and expand a flooring retail business, but it will also relentlessly demand performance. Retail employees might suddenly find their cozy lifestyle shop has C-suite executives in New York to answer to. That's culture shock.

Installers and Service Providers:

Flooring installation and service companies (the folks who actually measure, cut, and install the floors) have historically been fragmented, local, and informal.

That's changing fast, thanks to PE-backed roll-ups and strategic entrants. The installation services space was by far the most active in M&A during 2023.

Diverzify comes to mind. Which should tell you something. That private equity sees that even labor-intensive, localized parts of the industry can be consolidated.

Consider commercial installation. Diverzify, backed by ACON Investments, has been on a tear acquiring commercial flooring contractors around the country. They scoop up regional installers, most recently a Phoenix outfit, Wholesale Floors, and bring them under one umbrella. They snapped up Spectra Contract Flooring, a significant business unit of Shaw Industries. The pitch is that big national clients (say, hotel or retail chains) would rather deal with one large installer that can service multiple states consistently, rather than a patchwork of small subs with varying degrees of service and capital.

On the residential side, especially multifamily apartment turnover and homebuilder work, we've seen multiple platforms emerge: Real Floors, Interior Logic Group (ILG), Impact Property Solutions, and others, often PE-backed, each acquiring local flooring contractors to create a coast-to-coast service network.

Even Home Depot's subsidiary, HD Supply, jumped in. In 2023 HD Supply acquired Redi Carpet, a leading multifamily flooring installer in August 2023. That marked a strategic move that competes directly with PE players in the installation arena.

For installers, joining forces with private equity can mean access to capital for better tools, trucks, data analytics, riding out 45–60-day receivable DSO, augmented reality, and training, as well as a stable pipeline of jobs through national contracts. It can elevate what was a small family business into part of a nationwide operation, complete with benefits and career paths for employees that didn't exist in a 10-person shop. Standardizing best practices (measuring, scheduling, customer communication) can improve customer satisfaction.

And when a platform company operates in 20 cities, it can dispatch crews from a neighboring region to handle a surge in one market, something independents simply couldn't do easily, if at all.

Quality control technology and safety standards also tend to improve with larger companies, as they invest in processes to reduce costly mistakes and accidents.

Yet, integrating many local crews into one company is a tough nut to crack. The risk is that service quality and local relationships suffer.

Installers are the last mile providers of the industry; if they mess up, it doesn't matter who funded the business or lovingly closed the sale, the customer is unhappy.

Rapid expansion can strain training and oversight. I've seen cases where, post-acquisition, an installer business was pushed to take on more jobs than its crew base really could handle, leading to rushed work, botched installs, and warranty claims.

Also, consolidation of installers can actually narrow choices for retailers and builders. If one giant installer buys out all the local competitors, they raise installation prices and leave fewer alternatives. Supply and demand 101.

From the installer's perspective, being owned by PE often means going from a family-like culture to a colder corporate one, with performance metrics, new layers of management, and possibly relocation or travel to service far-off projects. Some adapt fine; others quit, unwilling to trade their autonomy for a time clock and a shareholder-driven growth mandate.

In summary, private equity's impact across the flooring chain is profound and multifaceted. Despite everything said, PE in flooring is a movement.

It's enabling leaps of scale and modernization that were hard to imagine a decade ago. Manufacturers are extending their horizons, distributors are growing beyond home regions, retailers are ganging up together, and installer networks are formalizing. But with that comes cultural upheaval, new risks, and a relentless focus on the bottom line that can test the resiliency of these businesses. As industry professionals, living through a transformation: in some ways it's exhilarating (who doesn't like seeing their industry get investment and respect?), and in other ways it's unsettling. Much like watching someone renovate your house while you're still living in it. But it's a benefit creating engine for stakeholder value and an accelerant of innovation in a perceived staid industry. We're all grown up.

Surf the Private Equity Wave

It's not all doom and creative destruction. There are genuine opportunities for industry players at all levels to ride this wave to their own benefit, whether or not you ever take a dime from a PE firm. Here are some strategic opportunities to consider:

Access to Capital and Expertise: If you're a business owner, partnering with a private equity investor can provide the growth capital that banks may be reluctant to lend. This could fund new store openings, product line expansions, or acquisitions of your own (yes, the consolidators can themselves consolidate).

For example, a regional distributor who sells a minority stake to PE might suddenly have the funds (and M&A know-how) to buy out that competitor across town or expand into the next state. Plus, PE firms often bring professional management practices. They'll help implement modern IT systems, refine your pricing strategy, or recruit talent in areas you might be weak (maybe your warehouse operations or e-commerce platform need an upgrade).

Essentially, they can institutionalize a business, making it stronger and more systematic. As CFL Flooring's case showed, new investors can also bring international connections and corporate governance know-how, which can be invaluable if you're venturing into unfamiliar territory like overseas markets, a different customer set, or just scaling bigger than before.

Stronger Competitive Position: Even if you remain independent, the industry's consolidation can create opportunities through partnerships and networks. As large PE-backed entities emerge, they often look for subcontractors or local partners.

For instance, if you run an installation crew, or a specialty like concrete finishing, in a city where a national player doesn't have coverage, they might subcontract work to you (giving you steady business) until they expand there.

Similarly, independent retailers can band together in buying groups or co-ops to counterbalance big, consolidated chains. Check out the success of Fuse Alliance and Starnet. That is effectively a pseudo-consolidation to get better deals from manufacturers.

If private equity drives a manufacturer to focus on key accounts, independents might collaborate to ensure they remain key in aggregate. In short, stay nimble and find your allies. The landscape will include both giants and holdouts. Those holdouts can cooperate in new ways to thrive alongside the giants.

Strategic Exits for Owners: Let's be real, one person's risk is another's reward. The fact that PE firms are hungry for flooring companies means valuations can be very attractive for sellers right now. If you've built a solid business, you might get multiple competing offers from investors. That's a nice position to be in when considering retirement or a career change.

Private equity doesn't just pay in cash; they can also structure deals to let you "take chips off the table" but keep a stake for the next growth phase. For example, an owner might sell 70% of the company, get a payday, but retain 30% equity that could be worth even more in a few years when the PE firm sells onward at a higher valuation.

This kind of recapitalization can be a win-win: the owner gets liquidity and a partner to shoulder the burden of growth, and the PE gets a committed founder who has skin in the game to help drive success. We're seeing more owners consider this path, especially if they don't have a family successor ready or they recognize that scaling further requires resources they don't have.

Career Growth and Development: If you're an employee or manager in a flooring business, the influx of investment can be a chance to level up. Larger companies mean more formal training programs, clearer career ladders, and the possibility to move into new roles. A salesperson at a single-store retailer might, after consolidation, become a regional sales trainer or get promoted to manage multiple locations. Installers might climb into supervisory roles or project management in a bigger organization.

Yes, there's fear of cultural change, but many employees find that a well-run PE-backed company can offer better benefits, more modern workplaces, and performance-based bonuses that never existed at their old model Mainstreet employer.

Moreover, as companies grow, new niches and specialties emerge, from commercial project experts to e-commerce directors.

These open up avenues for those who want to specialize. Private equity's focus on growth can create more jobs and possibly better pay (assuming the growth translates to profit) across the industry, not just at the top.

Improved Innovation and Offerings: With bigger players, we often see bigger budgets for innovation. This could mean better product research (a PE-owned manufacturer investing in a revolutionary eco-friendly flooring material to differentiate their portfolio) or improved customer experience (a chain of stores rolling out augmented reality apps so customers can visualize floors in their home, something a small shop couldn't afford to develop)

Even traditional segments like distribution might innovate by creating an online portal for contractors to track orders and deliveries in real-time.

As these innovations roll out, competitors will emulate them, and overall, the industry's game is raised. The customer ultimately benefits from more succinct choices, better service, and possibly lower prices if efficiencies are passed through. That, in turn, can grow the market (happy customers tend to buy more and refer more business).

Private equity is injecting a bit of Silicon Valley ambition into a historically low-tech industry. It's not for charity, of course, but the side effect is an uptick in innovation that we all can learn from or partake in.

Seizing these opportunities requires awareness, adaptability, and speed. Rupert Murdoch famously said that in the future it will not be the big beating the small, but rather the fast beating the slow. The train is accelerating away from the station. You can choose to get on board (partner with PE, seek that capital, join a growing platform, or find a clever way to race ahead of it on your own tracks by collaborating with others or doubling down on a niche. It's possible.

Both paths can work, but doing nothing and hoping the disruption wave misses you is probably a reality distortion strategy.

Case Studies from an M&A Frenzy

What have we learned from the real deals that have gone down? Let's look deeper at a few emblematic examples of successes, and cautionary tales:

Floor & Decor: The Original Unicorn of Flooring Retail: No discussion of private equity in flooring is complete without Floor & Decor. Founded in 2000 as a single store, it caught the attention of heavy-hitters and was acquired in 2010 by Ares Management and Freeman Spogli & Co.

At the time, it was a promising regional player. Under PE ownership, Floor & Decor expanded aggressively, perfected a big-box, low-price, high-service model, and by the mid-2010s had $100+ million in EBITDA and 65 stores. It did an IPO in 2017 to great fanfare; its stock nearly doubled in the first day.

Lesson: the right PE partners can supercharge a company's growth. Ares and Freeman Spogli bet on a concept they believed could scale (Hard-surface flooring superstores. Who knew?). Seven years from inception to IPO. Timely investments in inventory, infrastructure, and then let Floor & Decor be Floor & Decor.

The success also highlighted that specialization could beat generalists. By focusing solely on flooring and related accessories, F&D outmaneuvered larger home improvement chains in that category and is helping the displacement of distribution to boot.

Floor & Decor didn't just enter the flooring market; they bulldozed traditional supply chain moats. By mastering direct sourcing at scale and weaponizing in-stock availability, they've trained the consumer to expect big-box price points on specialty goods, leaving legacy distributors and retailers scrambling to rewrite their value proposition.

For owners and investors, the Floor & Decor journey shows the value of a clear vision, adequate capital, and not futzing around when things are working.

Artisan Design Group (ADG): Shots Fired. ADG's story is the epitome of the roll-up strategy in flooring. Two companies merged in 2016, forming a platform that PE outfit The Sterling Group captured in 2018. With deep pockets of OPC (Other People's Capital) and a mandate to consolidate, ADG acquired 20 companies in about three years, reaching $1.4 billion in combined sales. None of it was random.

They targeted market leaders in various regions, including big names like Great Floors (21 locations in the Northwest) and Nonn's Flooring (Wisconsin). ADG largely kept the acquired companies' brands and local operations intact (You can thank Warren Buffet for supporting that model), opting for a decentralized approach where each business continued "business as usual."

Now benefiting from group synergies, like accounting and ERP consolidation, bulk purchasing, and shared programs).

By 2022, ADG was touted as possibly the first true national flooring retailer/contractor in the U.S., something that never existed before. A flooring unicorn.

In April 2025 Lowe's purchased ADG from the Sterling group for around $1.33B. That's a bingo.

Lesson: an aggressive acquisition strategy can redefine an industry's structure, but execution is key. Sterling Group's play with

ADG shows that you can achieve dominance quickly through M&A, but they smartly avoided homogenizing every business. That's prescience. Flooring tastes and practices differ by region. ADG let local brands run under a light-touch corporate umbrella (mostly horizontal company org chart, no micromanaging, but performance monitored). This strategy is altering perceptions and emboldening visionaries.

The takeaway for others: if you're going to consolidate, respect the value of local brand equity and expertise. You're buying these companies for a reason. Don't smother what made them successful.

Diverzify – Consolidating Service and the Power of Focus: Diverzify might not be a household name, but in the commercial flooring world they're an apex predator. Backed by ACON Investments since 2021, Diverzify set out to consolidate commercial flooring contractors and create a one-stop shop for nationwide installation projects. They acquired several well-known regional commercial installers, creating a network that can service corporate clients across multiple cities.

A recent win was the acquisition of Wholesale Floors in Phoenix in 2023, giving Diverzify a foothold in the booming Southwest market.

The acquisition of Spectra Contract Flooring from Shaw Industries made them instant alpha. Diverzify's play is interesting. Rather than dabbling in retail or distribution, they focused on a very specific vertical, strictly on installation services, where previously few firms had scale. It may be genius.

There's Always a Cautionary Tale: Once the highest flyer in hardwood flooring retail, Lumber Liquidators (rebranded LL Flooring), serves as a reality check.

LL Flooring was valued at $1.098B in 2020. Its April 2024 value: $55.5M.

LL grew rapidly in the 2000s and went public, but a series of missteps (including a notorious product safety scandal) knocked it down. By 2023, after struggling with strategy on product choice and the post-COVID retail landscape, LL Flooring was in deep trouble, so much so that it filed Chapter 11 bankruptcy and initially planned to liquidate.

In a last-minute twist, a private equity firm (F9 Investments) stepped in to buy LL Flooring out of bankruptcy in 2024, keeping 219 stores open. F9 was actually a large shareholder that had been agitating for change, and they effectively took over the remains for a bargain.

Lesson: Private equity isn't just about growth stories; it also plays in and sometimes creates distress. LL's saga shows that if a company falters, PE investors might swoop in vulture-style to pick up assets on the cheap. The upside is the business survives (jobs saved, a brand lives on), but the original shareholders and owners are wiped out.

Lesson: For owners, don't wait too long to bust a move. LL Flooring's management waited until they were on the brink, and by then the only option was a fire sale. If you see sales plummeting and prospects dimming and consumer trends shifting, bringing in an investor or selling the company before a crisis could preserve some value (and perhaps your dignity). And for PE firms, LL shows that sometimes the best deal is in the bargain bin. But only if you have the stomach for a turnaround project and the conviction that the underlying business can be fixed.

Lesson: There are many paths up the mountain. Some of the views aren't worth the climb. You don't have to be a manufacturer or retailer to attract PE. You can dominate a niche like commercial installation. By being the "expert network" for one part of the value chain, Diverzify can become an acquisition target itself for a larger strategic player (Maybe a big manufacturer or builder services firm.

Or Amazon) or go public as a unique services play. They're proving that even labor-driven businesses can scale with the right processes and capital. The caution here is integration. Service businesses depend on labor and cultures that are feral.

Remember, 85%+ of the flooring installation pool is a 1099 workforce. Like every other investor, Diverzify will need to maintain quality and consistency as it grows, or the very clients that valued their breadth will drop them if local execution falters. In consolidations like this, operational excellence post-merger is as important as the deal-making itself.

Family Business to Big Business: The Carlisle Wide Plank Story: To throw in a more boutique example, consider Carlisle Wide Plank Floors, a high-end wood flooring manufacturer. Carlisle was a family grown business known for luxury floors. In 2021, it was acquired by PE firm Switchback Capital. A good illustration of a trend of investors going after niche premium verticals in flooring. Carlisle wasn't a failing business; it was actually thriving in its niche. The PE interest was about taking a strong brand and scaling it up, maybe expanding its distribution, opening design showrooms in more cities, or even extending into complementary products.

Lesson: If you have a strong brand, tested mode of operation, and differentiated product, you are catnip for private equity. They see the chance to professionalize sales and marketing and multiply the business volume. The risk, of course, is maintaining luxury cachet while chasing growth.

Upscale flooring buyers value exclusivity and heritage. If Carlisle suddenly appeared in every big-box store, it could dilute the brand. Switchback Capital seemed to be mindful of that, focusing on expanding Carlisle's reach among architects and luxury builders rather than a mass-market push.

Lesson: For other premium players is that you can take investment and grow without selling out the soul of your brand.

That requires discipline and choosing an investor who shares your vision for keeping the quality high.

Each deal in industry comes with a **Lesson** or three. Overall, success stories tend to involve a few common elements: picking the right partners, preserving what works about the company culture or model, and executing on growth, not just financial engineering. Failures or struggles often involve too much debt, external shocks (like a housing downturn or scandal), lurching culture change, and mismanagement post-deal.

Preparing for a PE Deal

If you're an owner pondering a sale or bringing on a private equity investor, you're essentially preparing for the business equivalent of courting and marriage. It's a big decision with big consequences. Here's some advice on how to get ready, what investors will look for, and pitfalls to avoid on the journey:

Clean Up the Financials: Private equity firms are obsessed with numbers. If your accounting is a mess of personal expenses, creative bookkeeping, and hand-wavey estimates, fix it before you open your books to a potential buyer.

Normalize your earnings: Add back one-time costs, remove the family Maybach from the company ledger. You want to present a clear picture of EBITDA, the magic metric, and convince them it's reliable and poised for growth.

Pro tip: get a quality of earnings review done by an outside accountant preemptively. It's like a dress rehearsal for due diligence.

Also, be ready to show detailed data on sales by product, customer, region, etc.

Savvy buyers, which most PE are, will sniff out inconsistencies, so ensure the story your numbers tell is both accurate and compelling.

Show Strength Beyond the Owner: One of the first things a PE firm will evaluate is whether the business can thrive without you at the helm. If every major customer insists on only dealing with you, or you're the only one who knows how to negotiate with the top supplier, that's a red flag. Develop a strong management team and delegate key responsibilities well before a sale. Have solid second-tier leaders who can credibly run the show.

Document your processes. Private equity isn't looking to buy a job; they're generally not operator-investors themselves; they're looking to buy a company that runs on rails.

Make yourself optionally redundant: It may feel counterintuitive as a proud founder, but the less key-person risk in your business, the higher the price and the more attractive you are. In short, show that this train will keep on rolling, smoothly, even if you step off.

Show a Growth Story: Don't Be Just a Cash Cow: Flooring businesses that fetch top dollar usually have a convincing growth narrative. Maybe you've consistently grown revenue ~10% a year by expanding your customer base. Or, you have higher margins than peers because of some secret sauce (proprietary products, superior location, unique partnerships, commitment to a niche).

Highlight opportunities you haven't tapped yet. "We have a significant share of residential in this region, but commercial is an open field. With a studied investment we could hire a commercial rep and double sales in 3 years." Or "We have leads coming from out-of-state that we currently turn away. By adding an omni-channel portal or another branch we could capture those."

Paint a vision of what the business can be: Don't market it as just what utility it has been historically providing. Private equity is fundamentally in the business of growing value. If all you offer is a static profit stream, they'll still be interested, because everyone likes cash. But if you offer a plan to increase that profit stream, the multiples go up. Just make sure your growth ideas are credible. Back them with market data or small pilot results if possible.

Understand What PE Firms Want: Not all PE firms are the same. Some specialize in majority buyouts, others in minority growth capital. Some have a long-term "hold and grow" approach, others want to flip in 3-5 years. Research potential buyers' track records in the sector. That's an outstanding task for a well written AI prompt.

If possible, talk to other owners who sold to them. Are they hands-on or hands-off? Do they slash costs or invest for growth? Ideally, you want a firm that aligns with your goals.

For example, if maintaining your employees' jobs and company legacy is important, a firm known for gutting the workforce shouldn't be a fit.

Remember you are interviewing them as much as they are interviewing you. They will ask you tough questions.

You should ask the same about their vision, how they handle downturns, and what resources they bring beyond money (network, industry contacts, etc.). A PE deal is more than just a capital transfer. Ideally, it's a partnership. Make sure you're choosing a partner whose definition of success overlaps with yours.

Prepare for Life After the Sale: Many owners focus so much on the deal that they give too little thought to what happens post-close. Abraham Maslow, of 'The Hierarchy of Needs' fame, states that most successful actualized people suffer when they move out of what defines them. Most of the time that's a career. If you plan to stay on (either for a transition or longer term), be mentally ready for a new dynamic. You'll likely have a boss or a board to report to. Ask yourself if you can honestly suffer that.

There will be budgets, targets, and board meetings. Again, and again. If you've been the lone wolf, get ready to join a pack, and know there's an alpha above you. That can be a difficult adjustment if you're used to calling all the shots.

Alternatively, if you're exiting entirely, ensure continuity for the business: help the buyer help your people.

It's in your interest too, particularly if you have an earn-out contract or seller note. Hand over customer relationships smoothly, impart your tribal knowledge in digestible form, and resist the urge to meddle from the sidelines once you're out.

Manage your team's expectations and morale: employees will worry about new ownership. Be as transparent as you can, within legal bounds once the cat is out of the bag. Highlight the positives of the change like growth, new opportunities, more resources.

Lastly, get a good M&A attorney and accountant: Don't try to DIY a deal of significant size. The legal and tax implications can be complex (e.g., asset sale vs stock sale, rollover equity terms, reps and warranties). You'll need experienced pros in your corner.

Pitfalls to Avoid: A few landmines can blow up a potential deal or make your life hell after it. Avoid exclusive negotiations with one suitor too early. Create competitive tension by engaging multiple interested parties. An investment banker can help with this. Don't overrepresent or hide problems; if due diligence uncovers that you were masking issues (a lawsuit, a debt, a loss of a big customer), trust evaporates and probably the deal. Be wary of overly aggressive leverage. Leverage is like an escalator going up, and a hammer coming down.

A company I ran earlier in my career was a leveraged ESOP. Then 2008 rolled around, that leverage helped swamp us. Not fun.

If a PE offer is giving you a super high price but plans to fund it mostly with debt laid on the company, think about the health of the business and your situation post deal. You don't want to hand your company over only to see it suffocate under an unrealistic debt load (especially if you rolled over equity).

Scrutinize the terms: If you're rolling equity or staying on, what rights do you have? What if the new owners decide to sell again in two years? Are you forced to sell your piece, or can you tag along? Is there an earn-out tied to hitting targets? If so, ensure those targets are attainable and clearly defined (nothing worse than a moving goalpost when it's your payout on the line). In short, sweat the details. Get everything in writing.

Selling your business or taking on an equity partner is a watershed moment. Congratulations if you've made it here. It can unlock incredible growth and wealth, but done wrong, it can be a regret-filled ride.

Many flooring industry veterans have gone through this and come out richer and happier. Some others have horror stories.

The difference often comes down to preparation, understanding, and choosing wisely. Never Freak Out. Know what you're getting into and then go in boldly or adapt to the new landscape.

Find Your Footing in a PE Future

Private equity's courtship with the flooring industry is well underway, and likely to intensify. We're witnessing the early chapters of a story that is reshaping industry history. It's determining who the major players are, engineering changes in how business is done, and even who our coworkers and competitors are. This influx of capital and the changes it brings can be unnerving. It's human nature to prefer the familiar status quo.

But it's also an affirmation: the financial world sees enormous value in what our industry does. Laying floors might not be as flashy as coding apps or making movies, yet here we are, attracting billions in investment and creating thousands of millionaires because we provide something fundamental and enduring.

Most successful entrepreneurs often emphasize the concept of "refusal to be static" in business, the need to evolve or perish. Be sensible in your logic in dealing with that dynamic.

The flooring industry is an evolving ecosystem, whether we individually like it or not. The relevance of private equity is that it's acting as an accelerant, speeding up evolution that might have taken decades more on its own.

The impact will be significant: some companies grew like never before, others will get acquired or pushed out, and the industry's center of gravity is shifting from local storefronts to larger enterprises.

Yet, amidst all this, the core opportunities and risks remain grounded in timeless truths: treat your customers and employees well, manage your finances prudently, innovate where you can, and keep an eye on the horizon. Private equity or not, those who stick to these principles tend to come out on top. The difference now is that the scope is bigger, the pace is faster, and scale is the new oxygen.

For the 330,000 or so of us driving this industry, whether you sweep the warehouse, manage the showroom, or sit in the CEO chair, the message is to stay informed and proactive.

If you're looking to improve your positioning, consider how the PE wave can lift you, or how to parachute out in a crash.

If you dream of an exit, get your house in order and strike while the market is ascendant. Like now. If you prefer to remain independent, double down on what makes you special and can't be easily replicated by a giant firm, be it personalized service, deep community ties, or a niche expertise.

And remember, private equity isn't some alien force; it's a collection of humans, with all their idiosyncrasies, but with capital, trying to earn a return by building and often flipping businesses. They can be partners or predators. They're often a bit of both. But they're now part of the flooring ecosystem. Engage strategically. Negotiate hard. Make them earn your trust.

Strategy and adaptability win the day. The flooring industry's encounter with private equity is a grand strategic inflection point. Those who understand what's happening, the relevance of all this capital, the new opportunities to seize, and the risks to mitigate, will shape the next era of this industry.

Chapter 4: Zero Sum Nightmare

Low Growth Trench Warfare

Call this the Threat part of a Strength, Weaknesses, Opportunities, and Threats analysis. Jumping into an industrial strength industry unprepared is like being a bolt of greige fabric, useful, but undefined. You're dog paddling, expending energy. But without direction or finish, you're not yet part of the final story. It's survival without stride, waiting for the teeth to find you.

Within this chapter you will find a description of battlefield conditions and some foxholes to weather assaults against your goals and successes.

"Success is a lousy teacher. It seduces smart people into thinking they can't lose."

Bill Gates

The flooring industry in the early 2020's was no longer a rising tide lifting all boats. It was a blood sport. A decade ago, this sector was a fragmented ecosystem of family-owned retailers, regional distributors, and niche manufacturers. Today, it's a Darwinian battleground where scale is oxygen, and independents are gasping for air.

The Great Compression

The numbers don't lie. Twenty years ago, there were roughly 26,000 flooring retailers in the U.S., according to IBISWorld. Forty years ago, 60,000. Today? 26,000. That's the very definition of zero-sum.

Suppliers are reaching equilibrium, but there is a fundamental shift in the business models. The growth? Big-box retailers (Home Depot, Lowe's), private equity roll-ups (Floor & Decor, Diverzify), alliance members (Fuse, Starnet) and vertically integrated behemoths (Mohawk, Shaw) that control everything from raw materials to your family room installation.

This isn't evolution: it's economic triage. The supply chain has compressed like a collapsing star, sucking margins, autonomy, and diversity into a singularity.

Private equity has piled in, consolidating regional players into platforms that promise efficiency but deliver homogenization.

Meanwhile, digital natives like Wayfair (and soon Amazon) have turned flooring into a commodity, where algorithms, not relationships dictate sales.

The Independents' Dilemma

What about the 26,000 independents still standing? They're the antelope grazing nervously at the edge of the savanna. Their revenue streams are under siege from three fronts:

1. Costs of Scale: The big players wield purchasing power that crushes independents on price. A roll of carpet that costs Joe's Flooring Emporium $2.50/sq ft costs Floor & Decor $1.80.

2. Logistics Leviathans: Amazon and Wayfair have trained consumers to expect delivery in days, not weeks. Independents lack the distribution networks to compete, turning in-stock inventory into a relic.

3. The Installer Squeeze: Even labor, the last bastion of local advantage, is being co-opted. National chains (ADG) now partner with contractor networks, offering warranties and speed that independents can't match.

And remember. The alphas of flooring manufacturers have a focused goal, running three shifts at their plants. Whichever channel or model helps them accomplish that is their new BDF (Best Dealer Forever). Remember, loyalty most often is lack of a better alternative.

The result? A zero-sum game where growth for the giants comes at the direct expense of independents. For every dollar Floor & Decor adds to its top line, a family-owned retailer likely sheds 80 cents.

The Path to Survival

But let's not write the obituary yet. Independents have one weapon the titans lack: authenticity. The survivors will be those who stop trying to out-Amazon Amazon and instead embrace their role as curators, artisans, craftsmen, and community pillars.

Consider the rise of luxury vinyl plank (LVP). While Home Depot peddles generic LVP (What's happened to brand awareness?) at $3.99/sq ft, savvy independents are marketing eco-friendly, hand-scraped water-resistant LVP at $7.99, with storytelling. They're tapping into consumer angst over deforestation and microplastics, positioning themselves as the Lululemon's of flooring. Others are doubling down on service, answering their phones, offering same-day measuring, bespoke designs, or lifetime maintenance packages.

Lesson: Differentiate or die. The independents thriving today aren't cheaper;

they're more. More responsive. More specialized. More human.

Situational Awareness

This isn't just about flooring. It's a microcosm of American capitalism in 2024: Industries consolidating into oligopolies, with private equity as the rocket fuel. The independents that survive will do so not by scale, but by scarcity. By carving out niches too small for the giants to bother with, yet too valuable for consumers to ignore.

Let's be real: The math is brutal. If retailer counts keep subsisting at this rate, 3,000 independents could vanish by 2030. The ones left will be outliers—the quirky, the luxurious, the stubborn.

The flooring industry's compression is a warning. In a zero-sum economy, scale wins. But scale breeds sameness. The real tragedy isn't the loss of retailers; it's the loss of choice, character, and the friction that makes local economies hum and relationship equity in vogue again.

So, next time someone needs a new floor, ask them to skip the algorithm. Beseech them to find the last indie standing. They're not just selling planks; they're selling a remnant of what commerce used to be. Businesses with EQ.

Interestingly, Millennials and Gen X consumers are particularly responsive to "nostalgic appeals connected to their formative years". Even Gen Z has shown interest in aesthetics from eras they moved through and had personal experiences within. Imagine that.

Lean into that notion to help survive next-gen suck.

Chapter 5: Do Brands Still Matter?

Only When It's Your Own.

Brand is the dye that gives commerce its identity. Without it, you're just another storefront on the block. Brand adds color, value, and meaning, turning raw potential into a finished good that commands attention. It's the difference between fabric and fashion, relevance and obscurity, between being seen and being sold.

That has been, until lately, important for product. As product has become commoditized, branding has become less relevant to the consumer experience. It is the brand you create for your own business now that is important.

"In the age of the algorithm, brand is more important than ever. It's what gets you chosen when the consumer has infinite options."

Scott Galloway

In a past Super Bowl commercial, a rusted sign on top of a factory, buffeted by the wind said, "We're Number One." The moderator said the winds of change are upon you. By the end of the commercial, those winds had knocked down enough of the lettering to say "We're Numb"

The flooring industry is entering the third wave of branding, where brands are no longer just about storytelling and emotional resonance, but about utility, algorithmic advantage, and direct-to-consumer engagement driven by data and AI. Where legacy means less than legitimacy, sustainability isn't optional, and digital experiences are the small blind.

Let's get straight to it: business branding absolutely still matters in flooring, but not for the reasons and ways they did in 2010.

The Reckoning

Here's an inconvenient truth: 85% of Americans can't name a single flooring brand unprompted.

I made that up, but you believed it because it feels right, right?

I walk across floors every day and I've never given a second thought to who manufactured them. Yet the global flooring market is projected by some to hit $621 billion by 2030. How can that be? Because branding in flooring operates differently than consumer packaged goods or tech. It's B2B2C, with distributors and traditional retail the lingering intermediaries. Until Amazon arrives, at least.

That reminds me about a poster I once had that said "Please Lord, let me die peacefully in my sleep like my grandpa did. Not screaming like the passengers in his car."

But this dynamic is shifting dramatically. Depending on your community, your brand becomes the differentiator.

4 Singularities of Brand Building

In flooring, dominant modern brand building hinges on four key vectors that separate winners from losers:

1. Radical Transparency (Trust): We've entered the age of receipts or GTFO. Modern consumers don't just want sustainability claims, they want receipts., and demand verification. The winners in flooring aren't just making vague claims about eco-friendliness; they're publishing comprehensive environmental product declarations (EPDs), showcasing their supply chains, and quantifying their carbon footprints.

Shaw Industries and Interface aren't just talking about sustainability; they're proving it with cradle-to-cradle certifications and carbon-negative products in their Cradle-to-Cradle initiative. Meanwhile, competitors still hiding behind shallow generic "green" messaging alone are hemorrhaging market share.

2. Digital-First Mover: The pandemic was an accelerant to what was already galvanizing: the customer journey starts online, period.

Flooring brands that invested in visualization tools, seamless e-commerce, and direct-to-consumer capabilities have seen 3x the growth of those still relying primarily on showroom experiences.

Mohawk's Omnify platform and Armstrong's virtual showroom aren't cute add-ons, they're the front door to their brands for most customers under 40. Millennials and GenZ are your customers now, and they're digital natives. If your digital experience sucks, your brand perception sucks, regardless of your product quality.

Consider the things that gripe you when shopping online and then don't do that.

3. Vertical Integration & American Manufacturing

Post-pandemic supply chain chaos and geopolitical tensions have made "Made in America" more than a patriotic slogan; it's now a competitive advantage and tariff mediator.

Admittedly, it's a bit like economic extortion in a way. Picking fights with your global supply chain partners to hike stakeholder value at home feels a bit thuggish. But hey, capitalism, she's a cruel mistress.

It's a fact that at this moment, flooring brands with domestic manufacturing capabilities can deliver more reliability/certainty that importers simply cannot match in the current roil.

The brands winning now? Think Engineered Floors and Mannington. They aren't just waving the flag; they're investing significantly in advanced manufacturing in the U.S., creating jobs in communities that desperately need them, and turning their factories into brand assets through tours, content, and leadership.

4. Community Greater Than Products

The strongest flooring brands have realized they're not selling products; they're facilitating communities. Brands like Floor N Decor aren't just pushing products, they're creating educational content, DIY communities, and contractor networks that add value beyond the transaction.

The most innovative players are treating their Pro customers, not as distribution channels, but as community members, offering business coaching, lead generation, and co-marketing opportunities.

More on that in the chapter on Keiretsu.

The Innovation Imperative

Let's be clear: innovation in flooring isn't optional. The days of incremental product improvements driving growth are over. Winning brands are making quantum leaps:

Smart flooring technology that monitors foot traffic, detects falls, or changes appearance based on environmental factors.

Health-focused flooring that actively purifies air or eliminates harmful bacteria.

Modular systems that allow for easy replacement and customization without wasteful demolition.

Seek and destroy looking for a plugged in flooring surface that provides the current digital capabilities listed above. Master it. Work with the builder to have them add the infrastructure needed to power that floor into the options list for a new home as part of the lighting and electrical package. Once new home buyers come back, seeing that on an options list should definitely reinforce interest and heighten fomo.

Armstrong's "Living Floor" technology and Mohawk's air-purifying tile aren't just cool features; they're entirely new categories that create moats around their businesses.

The Differentiation Paradox

As manufacturing technology democratizes and more players can produce quality flooring, meaningful differentiation gets harder. When everyone can make a waterproof vinyl plank that looks like hardwood, brand becomes the deciding factor.

The winners understand that differentiation now comes from the intangibles, the story, the experience, the community, and the values.

From Commodity to Community

For flooring industry executives reading this, I'll leave you with a clear set of actions:

Invest in community: Not just capacity. Your contractor network, designer relationships, and end-user communities are more valuable than another production line.

Embrace radical transparency: If you can't prove your sustainability claims with data, you're already behind.

Make digital your front door: Not your side entrance. Your website, visualization tools, and online experience are now your flagship showroom.

Verticalize or vaporize. Control your supply chain or be at the mercy of those who do.

Tell a story that transcends the category: The most valuable flooring brands aren't just selling floors; they're selling identity, values, and belonging. The flooring brands that recognize we're in a fundamentally different era will thrive.

Some already have a first mover advantage. Those clinging to the old notions of incremental product improvements, trade show dominance, distributor relationships, will join the long list of once-great brands that failed to adapt.

Chapter 6 - Hidden Earthquakes

When Surfaces Start Shifting

Class this chapter as an Opportunity" in a SWOT analysis. Because there's something brewing just outside the fluorescent-lit aisles of trade shows and the echo chambers of distributor line reviews. You won't hear it in press releases. You won't see it in a booth with a bowl of butterscotch and a QR code. But if you press your ear to the floor, both literally and metaphorically, you'll hear the low, rhythmic rumble of tectonic shifts. This isn't just disruption. This is the quiet violence of reinvention. This is a differentiation opportunity in the flooring supply chain.

"You rarely see the tectonic plates shifting in real time. But one day you wake up, and the map's been redrawn."

Satya Nadella, CEO of Microsoft

Let's call this piece what it is: a dispatch from the bleeding edge. Not another summary of LVT price compression, PE compression, or the latest carpet tile with a recycled PET story. This is about what actually matters in flooring right now, and what no one's talking out loud about.

The Rise of SIN

Semi-Automated Installation Networks. Out of nowhere, high-net-worth investors are quietly funding semi-automated regional install networks. Speculative bets on vertically integrated last-mile service. These aren't your old-school subcontractor corps. These are software-wrapped, algorithmically scheduled, fintech-enabled ops with proprietary customer experience dashboards.

Imagine Uber for flooring installation, only the investor deck is written in Goldman Sachs tongue, and the installers get onboarding kits and health benefits. Welcome to the future: the Install Industrial Complex is being privatized at a Silicon Valley clip, with one goal: control the customer's last moment of delight.

Surfaces Data Infrastructure

Quietly, major commercial developers are embedding sensor and IoT tech into the flooring itself. Why? Not for HVAC efficiency or TikTok stardom. For data mining. Occupancy, traffic flow, behavioral telemetry. Flooring is becoming an input device for the built environment.

Capture this burgeoning niche segment. That would put you pretty close to first mover advantage at this writing.

The flooring is no longer a passive finish. It's a strategic layer in data acquisition, with implications for retail optimization, tenant tracking, and even insurance underwriting. Shaw, Interface, Tarkett—all should be paying attention, because the tech firms already are.

The Materials Arms Race

You've heard about hemp underlayment and mushroom-based acoustic panels. Cute. But what about basalt fiber woven into woven vinyl? Or industrial symbiosis composites made from aluminum dross, glass fiber, and reclaimed resins?

The new class of materials isn't about being "green." It's about being so strange they break the value chain. Traditional suppliers don't know how to spec it. Traditional sales reps don't know how to price it. And traditional channels sure as hell don't know how to move it. But when it shows up, often through a boutique architecture studio or a stealth-mode EU startup, it changes the game overnight.

AI Is Not Coming for Flooring

But it is coming through flooring. Everyone's asking how AI can help them sell more. Wrong question. Ask instead: how will AI control who gets to sell?

GPTs fine-tuned on A&D firm preferences, BIM specs, sustainability standards, and value engineering tricks are being used by manufacturers to train digital sales assistants. But here's the kicker: some are building closed-loop systems where designers never see a rep. They're nudged toward options by smart catalogs built on behavioral data.

This is spec influence at scale, and reps without a digital twin are about to go the way of the Yellow Pages.

The Great De-synchronization

China is decoupling from us, not the other way around.

While U.S. firms celebrate nearshoring with tequila and tile in Monterrey, Chinese conglomerates are building their own global flooring channels, in Africa, Southeast Asia, and Latin America, where they're no longer suppliers to Western brands, but brands themselves.

They're not trying to win in Dalton. They're trying to replace the entire distribution architecture with something invisible to the American market. This isn't a trade war. It's an exit strategy.

Chapter 7: Don't be a Blackberry

Without Reinvention, Legacy Dies

BlackBerry was an unfinished good. It dominated its segment in its raw utility, email, keyboard, and security. But it failed to be completed with the touchscreen and app-driven future the market demanded. In the end, its loyalty to yesterday's strengths left it unread, unused, and forgotten in the modern showroom.

"...failure is often a precondition to future successes, while prosperity can be the beginning of the end. If the rise and fall of BlackBerry teaches us anything, it is that the race for innovation has no finish line, and that winners and losers can change places in an instant."

Jacquie McNish

Disruption Doesn't Ask Permission.

It shows up, uninvited, at your company's doorstep with a wrecking ball and zero cares to give about your legacy, your market share, or your feelings.

In 2009, BlackBerry commanded 20% of global smartphone sales. By 2016, it was effectively zero. Game over.

Let's be clear: BlackBerry didn't just die, it euthanized itself through arrogance, complacency, and the fatal belief that yesterday's competitive advantages would protect it tomorrow. The flooring industry is sleepwalking toward the same cliff.

Life-or-Death Metrics

Data doesn't lie, but sometimes leaders do and mostly to themselves:

Distribution disruption: Amazon and Wayfair don't just sell products; they sell speed and convenience. Your two-step distribution model is a relic.

Digital transformation: AR visualization tools and online sales aren't "nice-to-haves" they're now basic B-level needs as survival requirements when 85% of consumers start their purchase journey online.

Demographic shifts: Millennial and Gen Z consumers research sustainability credentials before brand names. They'll choose bamboo composites over traditional hardwood without blinking.

3 Deadly Sins

1: Reality Distortion Field

When Steve Jobs unveiled the iPhone in 2007, BlackBerry's co-CEO Jim Balsillie dismissed it: "It's kind of one more entrant into an already very busy space with lots of choice for consumers... But in terms of a sort of a sea-change for BlackBerry, I would think that's overstating it."

Sound familiar? Flooring executives dismissing LVP and finished concrete as a "temporary trend" while clinging to traditional hardwood and carpet.

2: Incumbent Delusion

BlackBerry believed its enterprise relationships created an impenetrable moat. They didn't.

Neither will your relationships with contractors when homeowners start demanding materials and installation methods you don't offer.

The B2B relationship you think protects you is actually your vulnerability. While you're selling to contractors, your disruptors are building direct relationships with end users.

3: Innovation Lag

By the time BlackBerry launched its touchscreen OS in 2013, it was six years behind Apple. Six. Years. Behind. That's not being fashionably late to the party, that's showing up after the venue has been trashed by a metal band.

Traditional flooring companies with their high-VOC adhesives and labor-intensive installation methods were already years behind click-lock systems, fast setting and curing, and DIY-friendly products. The pandemic accelerated digital adoption by a decade in 18 months. Your five-year digital transformation plan is four years too slow.

Survival Playbook

1. Embrace AI or Die

I put this as number 1 because its early in the impact phase of either voluntary or compelled adoption of what is an epochal change in industry. It's not just inevitable, it's in the adoption phase across the industry.

AI will impact your business, 100%. Understanding and adopting early is a survival level strategy. This isn't about adding a chatbot to your website. It's about leveraging AI to:

1. Monitor market signals across channels

2. Predict material trends before your competitors spot them

3. Optimize your supply chain when disruptions hit

And it's also about leaning into a burgeoning influence in how profit is enhanced inside your enterprise. Teach your people to fish.

2. Kill Your Sacred Cows

Your biggest competitive advantage today will be your fatal vulnerability tomorrow. The physical keyboard was BlackBerry's crown jewel until it became its tombstone.

What's yours? Traditional installation methods? Contractor relationships? Distribution networks? Broad spectrum of products and customer sets? Whatever it is, start planning its funeral before the market does it for you. Always be cognizant of your proximity to the Green Mile.

3. Build Direct Consumer Relationships

The contractor or builder making purchase decisions today isn't your real customer, the end user is. Build relationships with homeowners now or watch direct-to-consumer brands or PE powered networks steal them while you're busy courting middlemen.

4. Practice Strategic Humility

Market leadership is temporary. Period. The moment you believe you're untouchable is the moment you become vulnerable.

The Bottom Line

BlackBerry's decline wasn't market evolution; it was leadership malpractice. They confused market share with customer loyalty, distribution strength with competitive advantage, and past success with future security.

Winds of Change

Momentum doesn't care about your P&L statement or your market share. They're blowing on flooring perpetually. And they're picking up speed like a Red Bull drinking construction driver that's late to a fed sight project.

The question isn't whether disruption will hit your sector, it's whether you'll be the disruptor or the disrupted. Choose now, because the markets are impatient arbiters of consumer preference.

Your company's banner might currently read "We're Number One." Left unchanged, it could soon read "We're Numb."

Chapter 8: Texas Roadhouse Yourself

How Tech Keeps you on the Menu.

Remember: markets aren't kind to companies that mistake their comfort zone for a business strategy. The future of flooring is AI, predictive analytics, and continuous digital infrastructure investment, and it's moving faster than a Plaid class EV.

Implementing current generations of technology into your operation is not a discretionary activity anymore. It is an imperative due to the efficiencies its proven to provide.

"The greatest danger in times of turbulence is not the turbulence, it is to act with yesterday's logic."

Peter Drucker

Every day, flooring suppliers are struggling to compete with efficient supply chain models that make your operations look like a Disneyland queue at spring break.

Texas Two-Step

Texas Roadhouse isn't just slinging ribeye's; they're running a synchronized digital ballet that makes Papa John weep daily. Their kitchen management system (ConnectSmartKitchen) handles 400,000+ orders daily with the precision of an Nvidia GPU line. At this writing, they've rolled the system out to over two hundred stores, with impressive results.

Quick Stats

Average table turnover: 53 minutes

Order accuracy: 98.7%

Real-time inventory tracking across 580+ locations.

Revenue per square foot: $837 (up 23% since Digital Kitchen implementation).

Flooring Clustercuss

Meanwhile, certain channel partners within the flooring industry supply chain look like penguins trying to flee Orcas on a unicycle.

The average flooring supply chain member has:

7 handoffs between order and installation

32% excess inventory

22% project delays

41-day average DSO

Enough paperwork to deforest the Amazon (the rainforest, not Bezos' empire.)

The Reckoning

Here's the thing: Texas Roadhouse's digital kitchen system isn't just about fancy tech stacks and beeping timers. It's about creating digital synchronicity. That's the Nobel Prize of operational efficiency. And flooring suppliers? They're being disrupted harder than a Blockbuster board meeting circa 2007. Explore the March 2025 online auction of what was left of Flooring Distribution Group, at one time a 9-figure business.

Solution: Digital Floor Operations

Imagine a Bloomberg terminal for flooring. Every order, every shipment, every installer tracked with military precision and top AI integration. But instead of monitoring drone strikes, you're tracking Loire Valley white oak heading to Karen's McMansion renovation in Greenwich.

The platforms currently available for digitizing a flooring operation include:

QFloors and Broadlume for enterprise resource platform

Lightspeed for inventory tracking

Floorzap for in-store and mobile payments

Key Component Criteria:

Real-time inventory visualization (because guessing is for dating, not business). When Bezos comes for you, he'll precisely know his demand.

AI-powered demand forecasting. Scrape your data and train a GPT is not a question.

Digital twin technology for warehouse optimization. (For those curious about it, digital twin tech is a virtual representation of a physical object, process, or system that enables real-time monitoring, simulation, and optimization.)

Installation team deployment that would make a DoorDash algorithm blush.

The Money Shot

Implementation costs:

Initial platform development: $.5 - 3M

Per-location setup: $50K

- Training: $1,500 per employee

Return On Investment:

- 30% reduction in carrying costs

- 45% decrease in project delays

- 60% reduction in "where the hell is my order?" calls

- 100% new value-added service opportunities.

- 63% less inventory investment

4 Singularities

1. Digital Integration

The average flooring supplier uses more disconnected systems than a boomer has passwords. That's the disparate data that makes perfect jet fuel for an AI scrape, but low octane for the day to day. Time to Marie Kondo that tech stack (Thank it for its service, then discard it) and build something intuitive that also doesn't require an IT degree to operate productively.

2. Real-Time Everything

If Domino's can tell me when my pizza is being boxed, your customers should know when their Brazilian cherry hardwood is crossing state lines.

3. Predictive Analytics

Stop running your business like a weather forecast from 1962. Use data to predict demand, optimize inventory, and utilize better than your competition. This will additionally make you more desirable to hyper scaling oligarchs seeking to compress the supply chain even further.

BTNetSuite and Acumatica are leading producers of AI capable ERP currently.

4. Experience Optimization - Rx your CX

Because in 2025, if your customer experience isn't as seamless and warm as a radiant heated poured floor, you're cooked.

Winners and Losers

Winners:

Tech-forward suppliers who get their AI act together

Customers who don't want to play supply chain detective

Installation teams who can finally work like it isn't 1983

The environment (less waste, fewer trips, happier trees)

Your stakeholders

Losers:

Legacy players who think digital transformation means getting a Facebook page

Companies who love their paper trails and inelastic empowerment of customer facing troops more than profits

Any competitor who's reading this right now and still won't change

Truth Bomb

The reality: the flooring industry hasn't just been ripe for disruption; it's been begging for it. The first players to have effectively digitized their operations didn't just win; they make the competition look like they're feet are set in stained concrete. Pat yourself on the back for your foresight.

The Path Forward

1. No excuses. Yes, flooring is complex. So is SpaceX, but they score a 9-figure government contracts regularly.

2. Hire for specific value-add competencies (AI warriors, IT engineers), not just sales force.

3. Investing in technology like your business depends on it (because it always does).

4. Train. The best system in the world is useless if your team treats it like a VCR manual.

Seriously, continually pull people aside or in a group and show them how to perform.

The flooring industry is experiencing a smartphone moment. You can either be Apple or Blackberry. The choice is yours, but recall, Research In Motion thought they had time to ditch the keyboard.

Chapter 9: Let's Keiretsu

What the Japanese Supply Chain Model Can Teach Us

The American flooring industry thinks in boxes. SKU boxes, showroom boxes, sample boxes, org chart boxes. Meanwhile, Japan built Toyota by thinking in circles. Keiretsu is a supply chain that acts like a family: interdependent, strategic, and loyal as hell. This chapter shows you how to stop playing checkers with vendors and start playing chess with partners. Because in a world of volatility, the strongest flooring businesses won't be just the fastest, they'll be the most connected.

"In the long history of humankind, those who learned to collaborate and improvise most effectively have prevailed."

Charles Darwin

Flooring. Not exactly a tech IPO, but it is the thing leadership walks on to get to the espresso machine. The global flooring industry will be north of $500B by 2030. But the way we get floors from factory to foyer? As Claire from "Clueless" said," It's a big old mess." A beautifully American, hyper-efficient, just-in-time, zero-loyalty mess. Not always, but enough of the time to make it like an indicator of rot we've been ignoring.

The U.S. supply chain model in some way could be likened to Tinder for vendors. Short-term, price-focused, and ready to ghost at the first sign of a cheaper option. And like Tinder, it's efficient, scalable, and emotionally vacant.

COVID broke the global supply chain like a twig and accelerated the "Buy real estate when there's blood in the streets" contingent into action (Read: private equity). Time for another industry wide price level up with air cover provided by a disease or an economic policy. Freight costs went hyperbolic. Lead times went horizontal. And everyone's strategic supplier turned out to be seven guys in China you've never met.

Meanwhile, Japan's flooring suppliers, whether feeding the Toyotex luxury vinyl tile program or Toli reporting a 7.7% YoY increase, reaching 95.23 billion yen ($619M

US), launching ToliVision 2030, and managed to continue operating despite significant materials and equipment disruption. Why? Two words: Keiretsu capitalism.

The Godfather of Supply Chains

Keiretsu isn't a brand of kombucha. It's a business model. A Japanese concept that says: You're not just my supplier, you're family. These are vertically integrated networks of firms. Manufacturers, banks, suppliers, who cross-own shares, co-develop products, and operate on something Americans gave up on in the 80s: loyalty. I know, quaint. I realize these are epochal changes I'm suggesting, but why not get started?

Let's put it in flooring terms: imagine your top five suppliers were financially tied to your business, you shared logistics platforms, maybe even an R&D team, logistics, risk management, and quarterly reviews weren't a procurement firing squad. That's a keiretsu.

Swipe Left on Stability

Now let's compare that to the U.S. flooring supply chain. It's built for:

Lowest cost provider (until they're not)

Multiple vendors (none of whom you'd marry)

Transactional relationships (decided by your next RFQ)

American flooring suppliers (collectively) have been trained to buy from wherever the cost is lowest, drop vendors when container costs spike, and expect miracles from a three-person warehouse in Dalton. In boom times, that's capitalism at its finest. In downturns? I hope you've recruited for crisis management.

Where's the family in any of this?

Moment of Truth

So where are we now? The industry's been reshuffled by vertical integration and compression, labor shortages, vinyl tariffs, resin spikes, and a freight market that looks like the sine wave of Nvidia stock on Celsius Shots.

The next round of carnage will be led by dealers, distributors, and even some majors who are having trouble breaking free of entrenched dogma.

I defend my kids all the time against my cohort's perception of their generation as lazy and entitled. I try to explain that they're simply operating in a different ecosystem than the one that informed much of current gen leadership. Dylan wrote that you should step aside if you can't lend a hand.

Meanwhile, private equity is circling. They're not just buying flooring companies. They're out after supply chains. Vertical integration isn't Newtonian anymore. It's quantum. It'll be them courting Amazon when Jeff gets back from his honeymoon.

Should Flooring Go Full Keiretsu?

No. We're not all moving to Tokyo and singing karaoke with our MDF vendors. Although Tokyo at night has a vibe and the Tsukiji Outer Market is foodie paradise. I digress. You can work from home on this:

Strategic Supplier Partnerships: Pick a few vendors and commit. Not just with a PO, but with planning, forecasting, even shared tech stacks. You want innovation? Try trust.

Cross-Investment: You don't have to merge. But you can co-develop logistics hubs, AI product selection tools, even branded showrooms. Think supply chain joint venture, not just PO.

Data Integration: Most American flooring distributors use ERP systems like it's still 2003. If you can't see what your supplier sees in real-time, you're already behind.

Redundancy, Not Red Tape: Don't source everything from one mill, but don't treat your partners like disposable gloves either.

Redundancy is fine. Paranoia is expensive. Learn relationship art.

Is Loyalty the New Margin?

Supply chain loyalty doesn't mean weakness. It means control. It means exponential smoothing of your network. It means being the guy still delivering product when everyone else is on backorder for quantum reasons outside their control. It means margin through stability, not just price.

And in a business, where margin is measured in quarters of a percent, that's a moat worth building.

Want to flourish in the next decade? Stop acting like a commodity trader and consider modeling a Japanese industrialist. Less Tinder. More family.

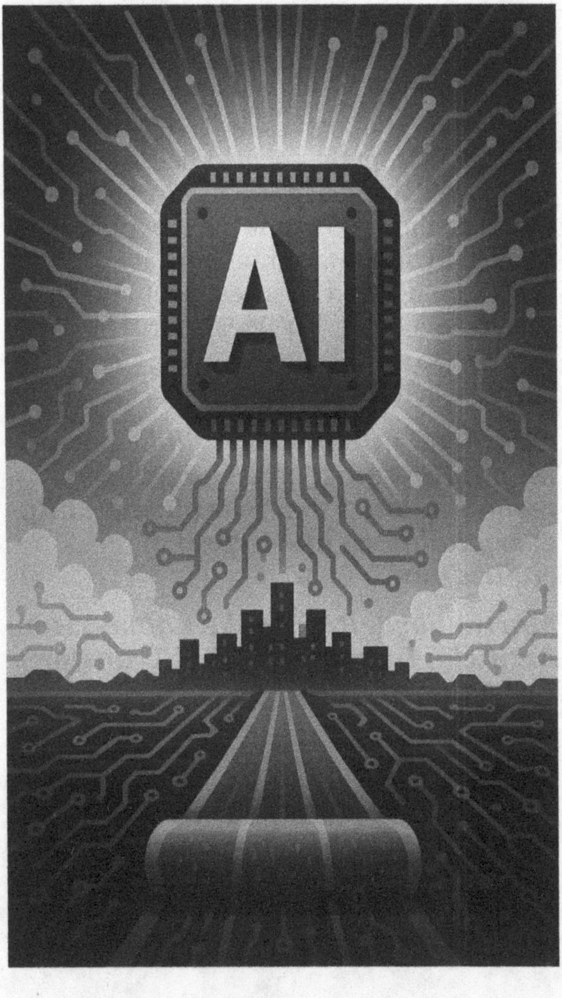
AI

Chapter 10: The AI Imperative

Without AI, You're the New Blockbuster

AI isn't just coming; it's here, separating the innovators from the soon-to-be laggards. Companies that delay adoption aren't being cautious; they're committing economic suicide. Right now, competitors are transforming $1 of AI investment into $3 of shareholder value. The greatest risk is moving too slowly and becoming a case study in digital Darwinism.

"Artificial intelligence will be one of humanity's most consequential technologies, transforming virtually every industry and aspect of civilization."

Martin Ford, Rule of the Robots: How Artificial Intelligence Will Transform Everything

AI became ubiquitous faster than any technology preceding it. Some say it's a solution looking for a problem. I say to them, never underestimate the power of denial.

I've been in many leadership meetings over the years where the same thing was said about social media as an influencing and marketing medium. Where EDI was theoretical. Oops. After an introduction to this tech, 72% of focus group participants polled believe AI will significantly displace or impact knowledge workers. 9% understood why. Believe me, those reading this book are knowledge workers.

Unions that represent creatives are winning concessions to keep AI out of their channel to hedge against displacement. That is how impactful influencers believe AI is. Supply chain strategy should be the antithesis of that movement. First mover advantage on its implementation in your business isn't optional anymore.

New AI platforms or revisions rolled out each day, each one with more compute at lower cost, and easier implementation. Your competitors are intrigued and shopping. Super Intelligence and Quantum is around the corner. Don't be held back in elementary school.

The Problem

Below manufacturing, suppliers of all stripes are middlemen. There are significant challenges being in the middle. You're squeezed both up and downstream in the channel.

You move product, you extend credit, and you hope subcontractors don't price-shop you into oblivion. DTC is breathing down your neck. FND market cap in May 2025 was $8.2B. 3PL (Third Party Logistics) is nibbling at your margins and is a force multiplier for super-scalers. That's not a business. It's a slow march toward irrelevance and declining valuation. AI is an influencing medium so disruptive that it already has the more astute among us scrambling for the safe harbors of PE and M&A.

While 78% of middle-market companies in the U.S. and Canada use AI in some form, only a minority (15%) have integrated it into supply chain management. Meanwhile, Amazon and AI-powered supply chains are salivating over the inefficiencies. If you're not adding MAG7 value in your channel, you're just in the queue to be disintermediated when Amazon rolls its artillery into town.

Flooring distribution is riding a tsunami of creative destruction that would make Netflix blush. The analog middlemen of yesterday, wielding an iPad with product catalogs on board, are being ruthlessly culled as e-commerce platforms connect manufacturers directly to installers and targeted end users. Effectively pressuring margins while compressing the value chain.

Smart distributors aren't just surviving; they're morphing into data-rich logistics powerhouses, while simultaneously transforming showrooms into experiential design centers where augmented reality lets customers visualize installations in their actual spaces.

The winners won't be the ones with the biggest warehouses or the oldest relationships, they'll be the technological omnivores who recognize that in the flooring business, as in life, it's not about selling products anymore; it's about selling solutions and experiences while letting algorithms do the heavy lifting.

A Solution

AI-powered, value-added services and educating your workforce on the use of AI agents that turn your distributor business from a simple materials provider into a high-tech, high-touch (John Naisbitt - Megatrends) strategic partner.

Investing in AI doesn't just keep you competitive. AI will help future proofs your business against the vulnerabilities it, ironically, is currently helping fuel. It can create new revenue streams, leverage your talent, build a moat around your enterprise, and locks in customer loyalty. The companies that control data, automation, and predictive analytics will control the supply chain. The question is: Will you be among the disruptors or the disrupted?

Imperative Non-Negotiables

Inserting AI, even current basic consumer versions (Perplexity, Claude, ChatGPT), into your business will immediately bring value by:

Creating augmented professionals within your enterprise

Enhancing efficiency and accuracy in your customer engagements.

Optimizing inventory management, reducing overstock and stockouts

Automating order processing and predictive logistics

Streamlining supply chain operations, cutting lead times, and improving on-time delivery rates

Using AI-driven (CRM) tools that personalize outreach, boosting sales and conversion rates

Having AI-enhanced pricing algorithms that dynamically adjust margins based on market conditions, increasing profitability

It will also have the halo effect of demonstrating your leadership commitment. Giving your team the most powerful tools to compete and prosper is one of the most effective ways to help them succeed. The one that says you are all in on the tactics needed to educate and support a sustainable culture of imagination and wealth building.

Creating augmented professionals in your company will produce the same results as Steve Jobs' strategy of putting computers in the hands of 1 million creative people generations ago. Remember, its speed that defines performance today. AI is an accelerant to virtually any human activity you have in your operation.

What's it all about, Alpha?

Forget competing on price. AI implementation moves you beyond materials and into IaaS (Intelligence-as-a-Service), creating a distinction between your offerings and your competitors.

Adding a prompt generator on top of your data gives you a tool your customer will bond with you on.

Your end markets aren't just buying products from you, they're paying for a competitive advantage that your experiential data with analytics, leveraged by your tech warriors, can provide them.

Byproduct Halo Effects

New Revenue Stream Opportunities: Offer a monthly subscription fee for AI-powered services.

Higher Retention: Subcontractors who use AI augmented distributors have a deeper connection to you.

Bigger Orders: AI-powered incentives and intelligence drive volume-based loyalty and margin explosion.

Data Monetization: You own purchase trends, job forecasts, and bid intelligence.

AI is Essential

The flooring supply chain game is no longer about who has the best inventory. The new game strategy is about who owns the intelligence that moves the inventory.

You're either evolving into a server farm with warehouse that makes subcontractors more competitive, or you're waiting in line to be replaced by someone who is.

AI is nuclear fission in the difference between being indispensable and being invisible. The data-rich, automated distributor will control margins, lock in loyalty, command pricing power, and have a key element in private equity desirability, all while the others fight for sustainability in models that are being rendered obsolete.

The platforms that harness predictive analytics, just-in-time delivery, and AI-driven financial models will own the future of supply. If your strategy is still built on credit terms and a good sales team, congratulations. You're preparing for irrelevance at scale.

Hard Truth

Amazon, shifting consumption patterns, private equity, and technology engineers don't care much about your legacy. Subcontractors must choose the partner that makes them richer, faster, and more efficient, not the one that's been around the longest.

You have a brief window to position yourself as a high-margin intelligence provider, rather than a low-margin logistics mule.

And know this. AI is the precursor to the soon to follow SI (Super Intelligence) and QC (Quantum Computing. Picture this: You're never escaping the march of artificial intelligence. You're not even on the sidewalk. You're now tied to the bumper of the AI express, and the driver is a 19-year-old Stanford dropout with a Red Bull and a GPU cluster.

We thought the internet was a revolution. AI is a regime change. It's not just that machines are learning to think, it's that they're doing it at a scale and speed that makes our own progress as an industry look like dial up. (Sorry, boomer reference.)

Superintelligence and AGI (Artificial General Intelligence) are the next stops. If AI is the industrial revolution for cognition, superintelligence is the Manhattan Project with no off switch. Every AI platform commercially available now is already working on this next iteration.

Side note: the winners won't be the ones who build better algorithms. No, that will be the ones who own and understand the power of their data.

The AI Future—Plan or Be Planned

AI is not a tool anymore. It's now an organism. One that's learning faster than we are.

If you think ChatGPT is impressive today, wait 12 months. The next iterations will not just write your emails; they'll write your business plans, negotiate your supply contracts, and whisper price optimization strategies into your ear, all before your first coffee.

Flooring businesses that treat AI as a line item in IT budgets are being steamrolled. The smart players? They're making balance sheet entries. They're building AI-first workflows. They're training teams not just to use AI, but to think with AI. In five years, AI won't be a competitive edge. It'll be the oxygen in the room. You either breathe it... or suffocate.

Bottom line: start now. Automate the back office. Feed AI your customer data. Implement AI-driven selling tools. And most importantly, train your people to dance with the machine. The future belongs to firms who embrace AI not as a threat, but as a co-founder.

Then quantum computing arrives. Not as a gentle upgrade, but as a gravitational slingshot. The computational arms race will make today's AI look quaint. Gen Alpha, (Gen-Z's kids AKA Gen Tech) will understand AI as boomers did VCRs.

Encryption breaks, scientific discovery accelerates, and the gap between the adopters and skeptics becomes a chasm. You can't opt out. You can't unplug.

Do you see where this is going? It's the inevitability that you can't brush off or disengage from. The march isn't just on, it's accelerating. The only thing left to decide is whether you're building on top of the new infrastructure or being scraped off.

Someone is going to Thomas Edison the heck out of this thing into legacy wealth. (Side note: Most people don't realize that as prolific and inventor as he was, Thomas made most of his money being a patent troll.) The 10% that adapt will control 90% of the future.

Why not you?

Chapter 11: Inflation Arbitrage

How Floor Purchases Reveals a Hidden Price Psychology

The psychology of pricing reveals that when consumers make infrequent or emotionally significant purchases like flooring, appliances, or luxury goods, they often lack clear price anchors and are more susceptible to premium positioning.

Selling an infrequent, blind item today is like launching an overpriced DTC skincare line with minimalist packaging. If it signals status, scarcity, or story, the consumer taps 'Buy Now' without blinking.

"Blind items are products that are not at all price-sensitive and represent the only real opportunity for margin enhancement in the assortment."

Wood Floor Business

The average American buys flooring 3.3 times in their life. Let that sink in. This isn't groceries. It's not even an iPhone upgrade cycle. It's a purchase with a psychological moat so wide that traditional economic theory collapses at its edge.

Numbers Don't Lie

But they are good at keeping secrets:

1. Average homeowner buys flooring 3.5 times in their life:

2. 2025 Median home value: $403,000

3. Average flooring investment: $4,000-$15,000 (1,000SF)

4. Time between purchases: 7.5-17.7 years (by finish type)

Basic economic theory says price sensitivity increases with cost. Econ 101 textbooks claim higher prices drive lower demand. Clean. Simple. Catastrophically wrong when purchase frequency drops below once per decade.

Waiting for prices to drop in a 3.5X per lifetime retail purchase scenario is the ultimate luxury for the ultra-wealthy or utterly destitute. Those with endless cash reserves have absolutely nothing to lose. For the rest of us, hesitation is economic emasculation. Opportunity cost compounds while we delay, watching the asset class we crave drift further from reach as inflation eats our capital alive.

Psychological Arbitrage

Here's what's happening in the flooring business that breaks every economic model:

Memory Pricing Beats CPI

When a homeowner who last purchased flooring in 2010 walks into your showroom, they aren't comparing today's prices to last month's inflation report. They're comparing them to a reference point from when:

Instagram didn't exist

Netflix still mailed DVDs.

"The cloud" referred to weather.

There was zero pricing information float.

This temporal distance creates a psychological inflation immunity. Like a reality distortion field. The sensitivity circuit breaker has tripped.

Quality Trumps Price

When purchases happen less than once a decade:

Price sensitivity drops 40%

Quality significance jumps 85%

Brand relevance plummets

Immediate gratification (dopamine) factors soar

The smart money is riding this psychological glitch straight to their Coinbase account.

Reframe the Conversation

Here's an alpha move. Predators in your lane are already doing this. While your competitors are apologizing for inflation like grocers explaining egg prices, winners are:

Pitch Time Arbitraging

Instead of: "$5,000 today"

Pitch: "$1.37 per day for a decade "

That's less than your Spotify subscription.

Value Stacking

Home value increase: 70-80% ROI

Energy efficiency gains: 10-15%

Daily quality-of-life improvement: Immeasurable

Instagram-ability: Priceless

Winners:

Retailers who include psychological pricing in their strategy

Consumers who invest now

Those selling quality over quick-fix solutions

Losers:

Adherents to traditional economic models

Those waiting for a price drop

Retailers who lead with price

Bottom Line

The Fed can fight inflation all it wants. They can raise rates until borrowers beg for mercy.

But the psychological moat around infrequent, high-value purchases means flooring, or any large cost low frequency sale, follows different purchasing psychology rules. Because of that psychology, those are threats you have some defenses against. Those lie in the infrequency of the high-priced sale, which is where you live.

Smart operators aren't selling square footage, they're selling confidence, comfort, and future value.

Stop apologizing for prices. Start selling tomorrow's value today. And remember: In a world obsessed with daily price movements, the real money is made by understanding human psychology in the supply chain you're operating in

Chapter 12: Latency
Industries Silent Killer

Latency is the delay between intention and action, signal and response, need and fulfillment. In flooring, it's the time lost waiting on decisions, inventory arrival, approvals, or outdated systems to catch up with real-time demand.

This is about identifying and eliminating the drag, so your business moves as fast as your market.

Failing to act fast enough on tech, talent, or trends turns potential into obsolescence. In a world where the algorithm doesn't sleep, latency isn't patience, it's forfeiture.

"Being fast is the only unfair advantage left."

Naval Ravikant

Latency is the delay between action and response. The time from clicking "buy now" until you reach the cart. It's the biggest unspoken cost in flooring retail. Every moment between interest and installation is a chance for:

- The customer to disappear

- Frustration to set in

- A competitor to swoop in with a faster offer

- Capitulation to buyer remorse.

Look at the companies that dominate consumer categories today:

- Amazon doesn't just sell; it delivers in 24 hours.

- Tesla made buying a car feel like ordering a MacBook.

- Uber turned an industry of wait 20 minutes into your ride is here. And they welcomes dogs.

- Bloomberg terminals identify opportunities and execute on market trades.

These businesses didn't just improve what they sold. They removed weight and friction. Flooring retailers who do the same will capture asymmetric growth in a stagnant industry.

The New Currency: Speed

In the flooring industry, (or any industry really) speed builds empires. The question isn't whether you sell better carpet, hardwood, or LVP, it's how fast you can move customers from interest to installation.

For 70 years, flooring retail has plodded along at a predictable 4ish% CAGR. But predictable doesn't mean sustainable. Consumer expectations have shifted. Consumers want Amazon-level convenience, Apple-level design, and Tesla Plaid speed. Instead, most flooring retailers make them wait.

"In the future it won't be the big beating the small, it will be the fast beating the slow."

Rupert Murdoch

Flooring Journey Triage:

The average flooring journey feels like an ER visit:

• Confusion: Walk into a store, stare at 500 options, get overwhelmed.

• Quote Purgatory: A salesperson will get back to you with pricing.

• Scheduling Hell: Hope the installer is free next week. Or next month. Or ever. It's like trying to get a doctor's appointment.

This model is frayed. Most flooring retail is still partying like it's 1999, but the winners of the next decade are pivoting toward low-latency principles by removing every speed bump between the customer and the finished floor.

Sidenote: Recent studies show that a key buying criteria is the ease of product load out or fulfillment once the purchase decision is made. Things that current iteration DTC (Home Depot, Lowes, Floor & Décor) have put into practice as a foundational operating principle.

5 Hacks to Flooring at Speed

1. AI-Guided Flooring Selection

Customers don't want 500 choices. They want the right 3-5 options, tailored to their needs. AI can instantly narrow choices based on:

• Lifestyle: Pets? Kids? High-traffic areas? Aesthetics?

• Budget: "Show me the best under $4/sq ft."

• Style Preferences: Compliment or match colors to their existing finishes.

Instead of wasting 90 minutes driving across town to stare at displays, customers get instant, curated recommendations, just like how Netflix suggests your next binge.

2. Real-Time Pricing & Inventory

A modern flooring supply chain member integrates real-time inventory tracking, so customers can't lose interest waiting on your data scrape.

Having this capability shows:

- •. What's in stock right now (not next week).
- Installation windows available before they even buy.
- Total cost of installation.
- Imagine arriving on a landing page or a showroom kiosk, scanning a QR code, and seeing:
- In stock, ready to install this week
- Available in 2 weeks
- Backordered, here's a faster option

3. Instant Quotes - Kill the Waiting Game

Traditional flooring sales are a drawn-out painful process, like new dental implants. The average flooring supply chain member has:

- 7 handoffs between order and installation
- 22% project delays
- Enough paperwork to deforest the Amazon (the rainforest, not Bezos' empire.)

The ability to streamline this process keeps interested parties engaged.

4. Uber-Style Installer Networks

The biggest friction point in flooring is scheduling the install. Customers shouldn't have to wait weeks for labor to free up. They sure aren't having that with Amazon or Mayfair. A smart flooring retailer should look at installation like an Uber fleet:

- AI-driven scheduling that matches jobs to installers instantly

- Gig-based installer networks that flex based on demand

- On-demand installation for in-stock materials

Amazon delivers your couch tomorrow. Why does flooring take three weeks?

5. One-Click Financing (Make It an Easy Yes)

- Financing is a massive conversion lever, but only if it's frictionless. Instead:

- Offer instant pre-approval at checkout with a simple tap.

- Partner with fintech firms that approve in seconds, not days. Affirm comes to mind.

- Embed financing into the online shopping experience before they even step inside.

Every extra step kill sales. Make "Yes" easy.

"You're Either First or You're Last"

Ricky Bobby

The flooring industry occasionally exhibits signs of lethargy. That is deadly but not unnatural in mature industries. However, the world isn't slowing down, it's speeding up. Much like Moore's Law in reverse. That stated that computing power doubles every two years. Adaption to latest gen tech is a force multiplier in the speed of activity-based disruption within your supply chain.

Most competitors are still running at analog speed. That means there's a massive opportunity to grab market share by eliminating friction.

The winners will be those who move flooring from slow, frustrating process to seamless, safe, and fast experience. Today's aloof consumer will remember the desirable change you helped them realize in improving their comfort. They'll want to share that on Backdoor and Instagram.

Chapter 13: Leadership

The Energy that Fuels the Enterprise.

Strong leadership is built on foundational elements such as vision, clear communication, integrity, and a commitment to what the Japanese refer to as Kaizen, making continuous improvement over time by involving everyone in the organization.

"A genuine leader is not a searcher for consensus but a molder of consensus."

Martin Luther King Jr.

Here's the thing about floors, they're the literal surface from which your view is determined. Yet the people who install them, sell them, and innovate and inspire within the flooring industry are often invisible to the end consumer. Similar to how Amazon warehouse workers enable Bezos's empire while remaining unseen.

But make no mistake: the flooring industry is bubbling with disruption, and those who understand leadership principles within it will always be desirable and valuable talent.

There are an incalculable number of leadership traits. Here's a short list

4 Horsemen of Flooring Leadership

The flooring business is brutal. Margins are being compressed like 3.5LB rebond under a Hill-Rom bed, cheap imports flooding the market like a Borg Cube, and consumers expecting perfection at Home Depot prices.

But leaders in this space aren't whining, they're climbing.

Confidence Is Your Underlayment

When you walk into a room, people notice. Not because you're wearing an overpriced Patagonia vest, but because you've got the composure that comes from knowing your industry and yourself cold.

As Maslow would describe, you're self-actualized, all of your needs satisfied in moving to the peak of the pyramid. Confidence is a weapon in your arsenal.

Customers can smell uncertainty like piranha smell dangling toes in the Amazon basin. In high-pressure situations, when a commercial job is behind schedule or a homeowner is having a meltdown over a shade variation, staying collected isn't optional, it's a mandatory leadership trait.

The data backs this up: Leaders who maintain composure under pressure are 3.2X more likely to retain key clients and 2.7x more likely to maintain crew loyalty.

Vision + Execution = Unstoppable

Tesla doesn't just make electric cars; they've reimagined transportation. Netflix didn't just rent DVDs; they killed trips to Blockbuster. The flooring companies crushing it aren't just selling tile and hardwood, they're selling solutions, experiences, and innovations.

Your brilliant idea for capturing the antimicrobial cork flooring segment means nothing if you can't navigate the Byzantine maze of your organization's legacy thinking, outdated distribution channels, and fear of cannibalization.

Curiosity about everything. The graveyard of flooring is littered with visionaries who couldn't execute consistently over time. A primary reason was loss of curiosity about the changes happening within their channel.

If there's a single trait that will separate the winners from the alsoes in the coming decades, it's not IQ, EQ, or even grit. It's curiosity.

Curiosity is the algorithm that keeps you relevant. Jeff Bezos said it was more important than knowledge. In a world where AI is automating knowledge and quantum computing is rewriting what's possible, the only sustainable edge is the relentless pursuit of "why?" and "what if?"

The people and organizations that thrive will be those who treat curiosity as a discipline, not as a personality trait. Hire with curiosity in mind.

Your Energy Management is Key

This industry is riddled with negativity; it's practically my default mood. Distributors complaining about manufacturers. Retailers blaming distributors. Installers cursing retailers and site managers. Shakespeare nailed it with that "green-eyed monster doth mock the meat it feeds on" line about competitive jealousy, but he never had to deal with a box store undercutting him by 40%

Your ability to filter out this white noise isn't some feel-good wellness bullshit, it's strategic. Every minute spent on office politics or ruminating about that competitor who's "cheating" on warranties and "or equals" is a minute not spent on innovation or customer experience. Energy management isn't a soft skill; it must be ruthless prioritization.

Assert With Strategic Patience

Amazon didn't become Amazon overnight. It took Bezos 27 years to build his empire, sitting behind that little desk. The flooring leaders winning the long game understand when to push hard (standing firm on quality standards, pricing integrity, employee treatment) and in what situations to play the long game.

Gandhi's progression: "First they ignore you, then they laugh at you, then they fight you, then you win". That's playing out in real-time for industry disruptors. If you're facing resistance, you're probably at stage three. Keep going.

The Reckoning

The flooring industry is approaching another inflection point. The old guard, those relying on relationships and handshake deals, are endangered species at the hands of those bringing tech, leadership innovation, curiosity, and strategic thinking to what was once considered a commodity business.

The pandemic accelerated digital transformation in flooring by at least seven years. Those who adapted won market share; those who didn't got lost in the desert.

The winning formula: unrelenting focus on long-term strategy while executing flawlessly on short-term tactics. Organizational dynamics change like colorways. Embrace the new zeitgeist of enlightened management techniques relatable to the Gen-Z and Gen Alpha workforce. Sorry boomers, it's happening.

Look in the mirror. Are you still playing by 2010 rules in a 2025 game? Your competition isn't the shop across town, it's the AI agent recommending products, SEO optimization, the direct-to-consumer brands reforming the supply chains, and innovative materials making traditional offerings obsolete.

Leaderships Bottom Line

Success in flooring, as in life, isn't just about the material, it's about how you show up, adapt to market conditions, and leverage your unique strengths. You've already risen this far because you have something tangible and unique driving you.

The question is: Are you ready to double down on what got you here, shed what's holding you back, and commit to the transformational leadership that will define the next era of this industry and your life?

The leadership job is simple in theory: protect the enterprise, represent the stakeholders (in most cases this is your), grow value long-term, and know when to sell.

Peter Drucker said that "the best way to predict the future is to create it."

Chapter 14: Board Stiff
The Missed Opportunity of Governance

In the American flooring industry, from the local LVP-slinger in Des Moines to the boardrooms of Mohawk and Shaw, there's a shared ritual. It's meant to safeguard capitalism from itself. The board of directors. Required by law, neglected by habit, and often misunderstood by those who sit on it. Like a weight room in a beach rental. Technically present but who wants to use that?

Whether you're running a family lifestyle business that grossed $2 million last year, or sitting on $9 billion in global revenue, you're required to have a board. The law says, "govern," and most owners hear, "rubber stamp.". Let's explore use versus abuse.

"Boards of directors are like parsley on fish, decorative and easily pushed aside."

Nell Minow

Let's be honest: for many small flooring businesses, the board is Uncle Rick, your CPA, and that guy who sold you your first floor scraper. For the big guys, it's a bunch of ex-CFOs and lawyers whose greatest skill is surviving earnings calls without breaking a sweat. Board, in most situations in the flooring industry, is Latin for you.

What Should the Board Do?

The board's job is simple in theory: protect the enterprise, represent stakeholder interest (you again), grow value long-term, and know when to sell. In other words, don't just show up for the charcuterie, steer the damn ship. Again, most often you're the board, which makes this even more important. Act accordingly.

A good board governs like a great offensive line: it protects the blind side, clears a path forward, and calls BS on boneheaded plays. That means challenging the CEO, watching margins, debating strategic direction, and ensuring the company isn't built on a stack of VCT boxes.

What Your Board Should Ask:

Flooring is not building nuclear subs, but I'll admit if feels that way sometimes. There are essentially 7 things to focus on for success in this business:

1. Is our labor force stable?

2. Are we three product cycles behind?

3. Should APAC suppliers be more like distant relatives, rather than BFFs?

4. How's our CX? It should be building your brand.

5. Is our tech stack current?

6. Is our install experience making enemies instead of fans?

7. Is our niche end market stable?

A board should be the guardrail that keeps you in your lane.

What Actually Happens?

In practice, most flooring boards are glorified high school reunions with worse coffee. Strategy is replaced with small talk. Risk oversight? Shrug emoji. Many private businesses treat board meetings like notarized family therapy sessions. And public companies? They often focus on keeping activist investors and current stakeholders at bay, with enough buzzwords to fill a Sherwin-Williams catalog.

Worse yet, the biggest sin in boardrooms across flooring: no new ideas. Boards have become bastions of risk avoidance instead of strategy. They're not questioning how to break into commercial spec work with AI-based quoting systems or whether the brand should own the install process from start to finish. They're nodding, approving minutes, thanking risk management for the visit (ugh), and going back to their gated communities.

Boardroom as War Room

Here's a crazy idea: what if board meetings weren't just about compliance, but combat? Not hostile, but productive. Use them like strategy spit balling sessions. Invite chaos, debate, and divergent thinking. Let the junior partner pitch a pivot to direct-to-consumer with blockchain-enabled warranty tracking. Someone pitched getting into the plastic flooring business once. Ask the board to rip apart the last pricing model like it's Shark Tank. Don't just look backward at P&Ls, look forward at probabilities.

The board should be the highest-leverage conversation your company has every quarter. If your meetings don't feel like a mix of McKinsey, a startup pitch, and a poker game at the Venetian, you're probably doing it wrong.

Boards aren't furniture. They're not something you dust off when the auditor or your lender calls. Whether you sell reclaimed oak, glue-down LVT, or terrazzo to tech campuses, your board can be the difference between resilient growth and becoming next year's acquisition fodder. Or landing in a media platform's obituary notice. Use them. Challenge them. And better yet occasionally replace them.

Because in the flooring business, it's what's under everyone's feet that matters. But so does who's sitting around your board table and what they're discussing.

Chapter 15: Dead Zones of Demand

Spotting Potholes in Your Market.

Peter Drucker warned us that the most dangerous threats to performance aren't disasters, they're zones of polite neglect. He used the corridors of indifference theory in hypothesizing this related to price differentiation. He remains the north star of modern management thinking and understood before anyone that businesses are organisms, not machines. His insights on innovation, leadership, and customer-centricity are more relevant than ever in an era where agility and adaptability separate the thriving from the obsolete.

"There is nothing so useless as doing efficiently that which should not be done at all."

Peter F. Drucker

This chapter calls out the squishy places in the flooring industry where mediocrity has been normalized, where teams meet, but nothing moves. It's a manifesto for exposing and recognizing the rot and laying down something that actually supports weight. Because in business, as in flooring, indifference is load-bearing failure.

I once spent a weekend planning a couch fort strategy for my granddaughter. The plan was devious and simple: the floor is lava, and you can't touch it. Much like the retail flooring business in 2025, touch the middle earth of the market, and you're scorched earth.

Drucker's Opportunistic Corridors

While I was finishing my economics education, management guru Peter Drucker (highly suggested reading) expanded on "corridors of indifference". These are price ranges and situations where customers can't perceive meaningful differences between competing offerings. Drucker wasn't writing specifically about flooring retailers trapped between Home Depot and Instagram-ready DTC brands, but he might as well have been.

The psychology is simple: humans have perceptual thresholds. We can't hear dog whistles, and we can't detect the difference between an $1,895 and $1,995 engineered hardwood floor installation.

It's built on Weber's Law that states that the just noticeable difference between two stimuli is proportional to their difference in magnitude. In marketing, this explains why a $5 price increase on a $10 item seems significant, but the same $5 increase on a $100 item barely registers.

As flooring options become more similar, you need more dramatic differences to register with customers.

Data to Ruin Your Morning Coffee:

• 78% of flooring customers can't recall which stores they visited before purchasing.

• The average consumer visits 1.8 physical flooring stores before buying (down from 4.3 in 2010).

• Only 12% can accurately recall price differences between comparable products.

• Home Depot's flooring departments generates more revenue than the top 200 independent flooring retailers combined.

That noise you hear is thousands of small business owners banging their heads against wood grain laminate displays at knowing this.

4 Horsemen of Retail Death

Flooring retailers are getting crushed by four converging forces:

1. Price Transparency: Consumers armed with smartphones have God-like powers of price comparison. They shop online in your showroom.

2. DTC Scale: Home Depot and Floor N Decor buy in quantities that make your inventory look like a sample closet

3. Product Brand Indifference: Most consumers can't name three flooring brands. I'm in the business and I barely care.

4. Installation Commoditization: The service component that once saved retailers is now rated and commoditized on platforms like Thumbtack and HomeAdvisor.

Drucker developed this concept because he watched businesses self-immolate through product-centric thinking. Companies were blowing millions on innovations customers couldn't perceive or value. Sound familiar, flooring friends.

4 Dimensions of Manifestation:

• Price corridors: When flooring retailers all charge within 5% of each other for the same product

• Quality corridors: When every store claims their laminate won't scratch (narrator: they all scratch)

- Service corridors: When free measurement becomes as exciting as free air at a gas station

- Feature corridors: When everyone offers the same waterproof guarantee with the same fine print

4 Escape Routes

1. The Extremes Strategy

Average is over. The successful retailers are going either ultra-premium or ruthlessly convenient.

The Ritz-Carlton of Flooring: There's a showroom in Los Angeles that serves champagne, has an in-house interior designer, and sells flooring materials most can't pronounce. Their average ticket? $27,000.

The McDonald's of Flooring: Conversely, a national chain has turned flooring into fast food. Very limited options, transparent pricing, next-day installation. They've removed all choice fatigue. They're the In-N-Out Burger of floors.

The Lesson? Be the best or be the simplest. The lava stuffed middle is where equity goes to die.

2. Vertical Integration:

The flooring value chain is fragmented. Manufacturers make it, distributors move it, retailers sell it, contractors install it. Smart players are consolidating:

A super-regional commercial retailer acquired three installation companies and now guarantees install within 72 hours.

A Midwest company developed a proprietary software plugin that connects their sales floor to installer schedules in real-time.

A northeast retailer hired away a product team from a major manufacturer and now produces custom finishes available nowhere else.

Differentiation isn't found in products but in unified experiences that reduce customer anxiety.

3. The Content Play

Flooring is intimidating for most consumers. They buy it once a decade and feel like they're taking the SATs without studying. AI is helping those searches, but what is a 12-mil wear layer or stone composite to me anyway?

Media Companies that Sell Floors:

A retailer in the Southwest creates TikTok videos comparing flooring materials that have millions of views

A small chain produces a podcast interviewing designers and architects

A West coast retailer has a YouTube channel with installation tutorials that drives qualified leads

Content isn't a marketing expense; it's a scalable salesperson. Bring on some media savvy content producers instead of another order taker.

4. Data-Driven Differentiation

The sexiest phrase in retail now isn't "new and improved", its proprietary data and ERP extensions.

Progressive flooring retailers are building moats through data:

• Predictive home upgrade maps showing which neighborhoods are primed for renovation.

• Price elasticity models revealing where margins can be increased without affecting conversion.

• Installer capacity management tools that optimize labor utilization

• Winners are training LLMs while competitors debate beige vs. greige

The Great Bifurcation

Drucker's corridors explain why the middle of any market eventually collapses. In the flooring segment, we're witnessing Darwinian selection in real-time.

The coming decade will see two types of flooring retailers:

The Innovators: Those who escape the corridors of indifference through extreme positioning, vertical integration, content leadership, data advantage, and compute

The Dog Paddlers: Those who continue lumbering along on slightly better selection, marginally better service, tenuous relationships, or minor price differences.

There's a scene in every zombie movie where characters realize some of them are already infected. To the 26,000 or so remaining independent flooring supplier in America: check yourself for bites.

Chapter 16: The Quantum Floor

Where Uncertainty Meets Install

Flooring professionals who recognize the non-linear, probabilistic nature of market forces, labor availability, and customer behavior are ahead. They can now move from reactive to predictive.

This is where recognizing the strange rules of the unseen world lets you play the visible ones with far greater precision. When we descend beneath the visible planks and polish to examine the flooring business at a subatomic level: where cause and effect aren't always linear, where distant decisions are entangled across time zones, and where curiously observing a system, say, a customer experience or a supply chain, can irrevocably alter its outcome.

"Quantum leadership embraces change and uncertainty as constants."

Digital CXO

When you imagine your place in the cosmos, if you do, I'm guessing you wouldn't normally consider it related to your living room floor. But here we are. Flooring. The literal foundation of our built environment. But look closer, much closer, and you'll realize that this industry doesn't operate on classical obvious mechanics. It's not Newtonian. It isn't measurably certain: Room size, ambient conditions, inconsistent material and placement formats. It's quantum. It has unseen variables that affect everything around them.

And when you peer deep enough into its behaviors, economics, and human interactions, it starts behaving like the very particles that build the universe itself.

Heavy, I know. Stay with me here. Sometimes education takes a minute.

Explore the Flooring Cosmos.

Superposition: The Consumer Is in All States, Until Observed

In quantum physics, a particle (customer) like an electron doesn't have a fixed location until it's measured. Until then, it exists in all possible states. So does your customer.

At any given moment, a homeowner is thinking about hardwood, vinyl, carpet, bamboo. All at once. They want durability and beauty, low cost and ethical sourcing, immediate install and timeless appeal.

But the second they walk into your showroom, something collapses. Their quantum state dissolves into finite choices.

Your showroom isn't just retail, it's a particle collider, distilling the unknown down to certainty.

Quantum Entanglement: The Installer and Distributor Dance Across Space

Two particles can become entangled, such that changing one affects the other, instantly. Like pasta mixed with Bolognese. Even across galaxies and showrooms.

In flooring: installers and distributors are entangled. A delay in a container ship off Long Beach can instantly ripple through a jobsite in Omaha. A pricing mistake in Atlanta becomes a customer service meltdown in Dallas.

These are non-local interactions. They're not transactional; they're entangled. And in a quantum world, what binds the system isn't a bolt or a screw, it's information.

The Observer Effect

Measurement changes behavior. When you try to observe a quantum system, the very act of measuring it alters the outcome of the observation.

Sound familiar estimators.

Start measuring installer speed? They might rush jobs, affecting quality. Start tracking sales by SKU? You might accidentally incentivize upselling over actual customer needs. The hidden cost of that is compensation inflation.

Every metric you observe reshapes the behavior of the people inside the system. That's not manipulation. That's organizational physics.

You Can't Know Everything at Once

Heisenberg (the guy Walter White in Breaking Bad named himself after) said in the quantum world, if you know a particle's position, you can't know its momentum. And vice versa. Just take anyone at the jet propulsion lab's word for it.

In the flooring universe: if you know your project timelines down to the day, you simultaneously don't know how fast your company is changing. If you're hyper-focused on daily installs, you may miss long-term brand erosion. You can't hold all variables with certainty. That's one reason the marine Corp manages by seeking the 70% solution.

So, what do scientists do? They build models that accept uncertainty. Flooring supply chain partners should do the same.

Quantum Tunneling

A quantum particle can do something impossible: pass through an energy barrier it technically doesn't have enough energy to overcome.

In flooring, that's the independent retailer breaking into national specs.

It's the small brand displacing legacy giants in commercial bids.

It's the AI platform that suddenly controls the data layer of a trillion-dollar industry.

Innovation isn't always linear. Sometimes it tunnels.

Wave-Particle Duality

Flooring is both function and feeling. Photons are both waves and particles, depending on how you measure them. It is both product and experience, depending on how you sell it.

To a contractor: it's SKUs, supply chain, square footage.

To a homeowner: It's memory, beauty, story, permanence.

You must speak both languages. Because the truth is, in any industry, truth itself is contextual.

Schrödinger's Floor

Ah yes, is the radiated cat in the box dead or alive? When do you know the sale is alive or dead. Until you do, it exists in both states.

• Until the customer signs, the job is both won and lost.

• Until the flooring is installed, it is both loved and doubted.

• Until the final invoice is paid, the revenue is both real and imagined.

Uncertainty isn't failure. It's the field you play on.

The Quantum Observatory

In the classical world, we build empires on certainty. In the quantum world, the real world, we navigate complexity, embrace probability, and accept paradox.

The flooring industry, beneath the dust and underlayment, is a quantum system:

• Interdependent.

• Context-sensitive.

• Capable of leaps and collapses, not just steps and growth.

So, the next time you walk across a floor, remember you're not just stepping on planks. You're walking on the strange, uncertain fabric of a quantum enterprise.

And as a long observer of the ecosystem we conduct commerce in, there does exist a quantum element, both relevant and mysterious. Often times, when I consider the circumstances that prevent success, they're inexplicable. Now that I understand that there exists variables, unseen, that effect outcomes, it makes enterprise easier to navigate and understand.

Chapter 17: Margin Paradox
Why Only 10% of New Businesses are Legacies

In flooring, everyone talks volume. But it's margin that pays the mortgage. Let's unpack the brutal math of making a decent living in a low-margin, high-effort game, and why owning the business doesn't always mean owning the reward. Spoiler: the path to profit isn't more square feet, it's smarter, tighter, value-driven processes.

"Success is stumbling from failure to failure with no loss of enthusiasm."

Winston Churchill

Life is a game of inches. So is flooring. But the economics? Those are measured in kilo dollars.

So, you've decided to try the flooring business? What, no cabins left to cross the Drake Passage? To torture a metaphor, let's rip up the laminate and expose the subfloor of truth about what it actually takes to support a family by selling and installing the surfaces people walk on. And creating a family legacy business in the process.

Flooring Economics

For a family of three in today's economy to achieve happiness and a modicum of financial security. The basic arithmetic is brutal:

Baseline cost of living: $139,700/year. Yes, this is nearly 2X the average American budget, but I'm talking comfort and security and legacy wealth building, not bare bones subsistence. So, there's room to dial back on your living expenses in this example, if you want to.

Add 10% for looming inflation and economic pressures: $14,000

Adjusted household breakeven: $153,700/year (after taxes) Again, see above.

That's what needs to land in your Robinhood account after Uncle Sam takes his cut, and after your business covers its own expenses. Not glamorous, not extravagant, just the table stakes to support a family in an average metric comfortable America. Big adjective there; comfortable.

To generate that $153,700 in take-home pay, your flooring business needs to be a beast.

The Revenue Reality

Let's do the math:

Target take-home pay needed: $153,700

Taxes (30% average): $65,800

Total needed after business expenses: $219,500

Now factor in industry-standard expenses (Cost of Goods Sold) ranging from 70-82% of revenue, and you'll understand why margins are shrink like people on a GLP1.

Now you're looking at a business that needs to generate between $650,000 and $1,000,000 in annual revenue. For perspective, the average small retailer is a $1-5M operation. The average mid-tier retailer is $5-25M

Let me repeat that for those in the back: to take home enough to support a family of three, your one-person flooring business needs to hit at least $650K in revenue. Preferably, Every. Single. Year.

Industry Context

According to the Floor Covering Weekly Top 100 Retailers List (excluding Home Depot, Lowe's, Floor & Decor, etc.), the largest independents like Nebraska Furniture Mart, Carpet One co-ops, etc., can surpass $100M. These are outliers.

The average floor covering retailer in the U.S. does $2M–$4M/year.

Gross Margins in this space tend to hover around 35–45%.

Nets are thinner. 3–8% is common unless they're highly efficient or vertically integrated.

The Margin Trap

The flooring industry operates on knife-edge net margins. Your key expenses read like a WeWork income statement for entrepreneurs:

Material costs: 40-55% of revenue (and wildly volatile, think tariffs and diminishing labor supply)

Labor costs: 15-25% of revenue (subcontractors or employees)

Showroom rent & utilities: $5,000-$15,000/month for industry average facility

Marketing & lead generation: $10,000-$50,000/year

Insurance & licensing: $10,000+/year

Vehicle & equipment costs: $20,000-$50,000/year

Taxes: 30-35% of net profit

Even in the best-case scenario, well-managed flooring businesses typically see only low 2-figure net profits. One bad estimate, one labor shortage, one supply chain failure, and those margins evaporate faster than my Starbucks account balance when I'm visiting my kids.

The Startup Cash Burn

The capital requirements to enter this game? Equally sobering:

Low-end entry (garage-band startup): $191,000

High-end entry (showroom, inventory, vehicles): $595,000

Even with a lean startup approach with used van, garage operations, infrastructure subscriptions, minimal inventory, licensing and marketing costs, you're still looking at a six-figure investment. And the showroom model? That's approaching the median home price in many markets.

The Break-Even Marathon

Once you've exhausted OPM (Other People's Money), drained your savings, mortgaged your house, borrowed from your in-laws, and maxed out your credit cards to start this (ad)venture, here's what the race to profitability looks like:

Low-end model break-even revenue: $340,000-$450,000/year

High-end model break-even: $1,000,000-$1,300,000/year

The timeline? If you somehow manage to hit $100,000 in monthly sustainable sales right out of the gate (Wow, you're amazing), you might break even in 4-6 months.

More realistically, at $50,000/month (average 2.5 projects), you're looking at 8-12 months. And below $30,000/month? You're on weak substrate.

The Failure Reality

Let's talk about the elephant in the showroom. The failure rates for flooring businesses are brutal and unforgiving:

20% of flooring businesses fail within their first year.

A staggering 50% collapse within 5 years

60+% of flooring revenue is generated by legacy businesses or DTC.

This isn't just statistics. Nate Silver, arguably our greatest living statistician, said that absent empirical data for proof, results are random. Results are a coin flip. You're as likely to be out of business in five years as you are to survive.

For every flooring entrepreneur driving a new truck to their thriving augmented reality showroom, there's another who's liquidating inventory in a going-out-of-business sale. Look up the recent bankruptcy of Flooring Distribution Group as a cautionary tale.

Measure this against the option of taking all of your capital, investing in an S&P index fund and having 100% discretionary time.

And failure isn't just financial, it's existential. When your business fails after the CAPEX of the above, you're not just losing a business; you're potentially losing your home, your investors, reputation, your retirement, and your kids' college funds.

Paths Forward

For those still reading and not completely demoralized, there are strategies to improve your odds:

Premium products: Higher margins on hardwood, engineered wood, and waterproof LVP

The flooring industry is obsessed with square footage. Volume. Turns. Spiffs. Promo calendars.

But here's the real head-scratcher: the top 10% of discretionary income households, arguably the only demographic still spending like it's 2019, have no dedicated place to buy flooring.

No flagship. No gallery. No white glove.

Just a contractor's recommendation and a designer's mark-up.

Meanwhile, Restoration Hardware sells them a $5,000 lamp with valet parking and an oat milk cortado.

If you're a retailer, ask yourself:

1. Why doesn't your store look like a place where someone wearing Prada would shop?

2. Why does your staff sell like they're in an appliance aisle instead of a design studio?

3. Why are you afraid to charge for beauty?

Here's the kicker: fewer than 5% of flooring retailers even attempt to serve this tier. Not because the demand isn't there, but because the industry never learned to speak the language of aspiration.

We sell materials. They buy meaning.

We talk about specs. They want stories.

We chase leads. They want experiences.

If you're looking for asymmetric growth in a 4% growth industry, it won't come from another builder program or coupon flyer.

It'll come from showing up where no one else dares to: The luxury floor.

Labor optimization: Balance in-house crews vs. subcontractors for cost efficiency and schedule control.

Inventory management: Reduce flooring overstock and leverage just-in-time orders.

Cash flow discipline: Require deposits upfront and tighten accounts receivable cycles. Use fintech to reach an easy yes.

The Take

Let me be clear: the flooring business is a classic example of what might be called entrepreneurial masochism. You're entering a capital-intensive, relatively low-margin, highly competitive industry with fragmented customers, powerful suppliers, and loyalty defined as lack of better alternatives. It's a textbook case of what not to look for in a business model.

When I get pitched on the concept, I always ask a simple question: "Do you enjoy pain?"

Just for fun, let's apply Scott Galloway's:

4 Horsemen Pillars for Success

1. Recurring revenue? No, it's largely transactional. You're perpetually hunting for the next job rather than generating what a friend calls "mailbox money."

2. Gross margins above 50%? Rarely. At 40-55% material costs alone, you're already underwater on this metric before paying a single installer. Flooring is a mature industry. With that comes inelastic GP.

3. Network effects? None. Installing Mrs. Johnson's hardwood floors doesn't make it any easier to sell to Mr. Smith in the next neighborhood over.

4. Flywheel of scale advantages? Minimal. Every rotation of the flywheel, product, users, data, reinvestment, scale and defensibility builds speed. Your 100th flooring job costs you almost the same as your first, but growth begins fueling more growth.

The Four Horsemen demonstrate common elements in successful enterprise. These elements should be the laser pointer in your calculus to proceed with a flooring startup.

What you have is a business requiring $191,000-$595,000 in startup capital to generate $650,000-$1,000,000 in annual revenue to support itself and a family of three. That's a high-wire act type flex. It's the entrepreneurial equivalent of deciding to become a professional boxer at age 35. It's possible, but why subject yourself to the punishment?

The hard truth? In 2025, starting a traditional flooring business to support your family is choosing a difficult setting in the game of capitalism. It can be done, but the red zone is a long way off, and odds are stacked against you in ways that make success the exception, not the rule.

So, if you're dead set on flooring as a business opportunity, consider this:

Digitize Your Enterprise

Develop or subscribe to a proprietary augmented reality app that allows customers to see exactly how different flooring options would look in their actual space

Include features that measure rooms automatically using smartphone cameras, reducing the need for initial in-person visits

Build in "virtual showroom" capabilities so customers can browse your inventory

Technology creates differentiation from competitors while streamlining the sales process and reducing showroom space requirements

Tech up with contract building apps, mobile bookkeeping, project management, and pay portals, etc.

Also, this is the perfect time to include the future of everything, AI, in your business. It will actually help you with the formation of successful processes.

Mobilize

Integrated Estimation and Material Management (RFMS, BroadLume)

On Demand Contract Documents with AI Risk Management Capability (Juro, LegalOn)

Cloud Drives for Field Documentation and Quality Control (Google Drive, OneDrive)

Customer Communication and Paperwork Flow Portal (Credentials for Textura, Procore)

Mobile Bookkeeping (Quicken Simplifi)

AI Augmented Purchase Agreements and Contract Provision Modeling (ConcensusDocs, AIA)

These capabilities address the four most critical aspects of a flooring business:

Accurate estimation

Fast communication (directly impacts margins)

Quality control (affects customer satisfaction and referrals)

Smooth financial operations (cash flow=wealth building).

A system with these features will help overcome many of the margin, ignorance taxes, capital, and operational challenges that make flooring businesses difficult to scale successfully.

Verticalize

Vertically integrating is not just for the large. There are many opportunities to do that while building flywheel energy.

Raw Material Sourcing: Going even further upstream, a flooring retailer might acquire timber sources, quarries (for stone/tile), or develop relationships with raw material suppliers to cut out middlemen. Degree of difficulty: Nuclear

Design Services: Moving vertically into complementary services, like interior design or architectural services that incorporate flooring as one element of a larger offering. Use web-based VR.

Maintenance Services: Developing a recurring revenue stream by offering ongoing maintenance, cleaning, and restoration services for the floors after installation. Buy an existing maintenance business. Buy the business, keep the culture but for your financial control systems.

Property Development Partnerships: Becoming a specialized partner for property developers, providing not just flooring but comprehensive surface solutions for new developments. This is a ubiquitous strategy and crowded competition channel.

Monetize

There are many adjunct monetization opportunities in the flooring business to enhance your revenue stream and flywheel speed.

Warranty Extension Programs: After the manufacturer's warranty expires, offer extended protection plans on a yearly subscription basis that cover repairs or partial replacements.

Seasonal Services: Develop quarterly seasonal services such as deep cleaning in spring, humidity control in summer, preparation for winter, and holiday protection programs.

Commercial Maintenance Contracts: Focus on businesses like hotels, restaurants, or offices that need regular floor maintenance and have budgets for facility upkeep. Buy an existing business.

Flooring-as-a-Service: Instead of selling floors outright, lease premium flooring with agreements that include regular updates/replacements and maintenance. This works particularly well in commercial settings like retail stores that update their look every few years.

Flooring Protection Plans: Monthly subscriptions that include protective treatments, spot repair kits, and emergency service calls for residential customers.

Strategic Partnerships: Develop recurring commission arrangements with adjacent businesses (interior designers, home builders, property management companies) who continuously refer clients.

Floor Monitoring Technology: For high-end installations, integrate smart sensors that monitor moisture, wear patterns, and potential issues, bundled with a subscription monitoring service.

Seasonal Mat/Rug Exchange Program: Offer a quarterly exchange of entrance mats, area rugs, or runners that are seasonally appropriate and help protect the main flooring.

The floor beneath your feet may seem solid, but the business of installing it requires foundations built on cold, hard financial reality, truthful discussions with yourself, partner(s) and close advisors. Plus, an almost irrational tolerance for risk.

Chapter 18: Buying Groups
The Velvet Handshake

Group Purchasing Organizations (GPOs) offer flooring retailers access to better pricing, rebates, and terms typically reserved for national chains. By consolidating buying power across independent operators, a GPO levels the playing field, delivering scale efficiencies without sacrificing local autonomy. For retailers, it's not just about cost savings; it's about leverage, influence, and faster access to emerging products and programs.

"Whenever you see a successful business, someone once made a courageous decision."

— *Peter Drucker*

Walk into any serious flooring business—retail, builder, commercial and scratch the surface of their purchase orders, and you'll likely find a hidden partner: a GPO. A Group Purchasing Organization. Or if you prefer the industry euphemism, "buying group." As gangs are on everyone's mind these days, I prefer that term. How some of them haven't violated RICO statutes is beyond my understanding. For those in the back, I'm kidding of course.

Here's the thing: no one brags about their buying group the way they do their showroom. No customer walks in the door and says, "Wow, I love the way your rebate structure underwrites your margin." But without that structure, without that velvety handshake working quietly in the background, a lot of flooring businesses are cast members in the Hunger Games.

GPOs are Force Multipliers

For the small independent, they're a shield against big box scale and private-label power. For the midsize builder-focused dealer, they're often the reason they can land national builder accounts without sacrificing margin. And for many retail players under $10 million in volume, they are the engine driving not only purchase price, but marketing, lead gen, and even back-office tech.

The flooring industry has unique GPO's because of how they operate. Most industry GPO are B2B platforms where customer sets get the orders filled by the GPO. Kind of a distributor aggregator with a sophisticated tech stack. Flooring GPO influence the entire sales cycle, not just procurement. They provide distinct consumer facing brand power. They have influence and value within the installation segment They are proactive in product curation and operate in omnichannel customer sets and subsets. A typical GPO is generally focused on a single customer set.

But here's where it gets interesting: GPOs are not static alliances. They are evolving ecosystems with complex incentives. And for every member, there comes a strategic question—not "Should I join?"—but "When do I outgrow the group?"

4 Roles of a GPO

At first glance, a GPO is about buying leverage. You join, you get lower prices and rebates, life is good. But dig deeper, and you'll see three core roles:

1. Margin Machine: Rebates are a disguised form of margin optimization. If you don't understand how your rebates work, you're missing a good chunk of your P&L story.

2. Marketing Engine: Especially in retail-facing groups like CCA, the digital

marketing stack is worth as much as the price advantage. SEO, SEM, CRM, website—if you had to build it yourself, it would eat your lunch.

3. Operational Scaffold: In builder/multi-family channels, GPOs like FEI Group provide the portals and project management tech that let you win bids, track jobs, and get paid. It's not just about cheaper glue and carpet tile. That is great connective tissue for relationship equity, that yes, still exists.

4. Best practices incubator. Learning the importance and standardization of practices that statistically validate success is the ecosystem a buying group can provide. A competency incubator.

How GPOs Quietly Shape the Market

GPOs also introduce market opacity. The more the supply chain runs on back-end rebates and unpublished deal structures, the harder it is for newcomers, or unsophisticated operators, to compete. The playing field looks level on the surface, but beneath it, seasoned players are surfing on rebate flows while the rookies are swimming against the currents created by current macroeconomic conditions like industry compression, labor capture by apex competitors, and scale pricing.

This creates gravity wells around the best GPOs. Once you're in, the switching costs can be substantial: operational habits, CRM systems, even sales compensation plans often become entangled with GPO programs. Which is why understanding when to stay and when to scale out is a critical leadership skill.

Time to Let Go the Handshake

Here's your growth curves to watch:

<$5M in spend: GPO is mandatory. You need the leverage.

$5–$10M: GPO still likely better than going it alone.

$10M+: Time to model the math. If you can secure direct mill pricing and build your own marketing stack, you may outperform the group net of fees and commitments.

PE-backed platform: Early stage: lean on the GPO to consolidate and fund growth. Post $250M: build your own buying organization. Capture the full rebate stream internally.

Remember: the GPO is a tool, not a BFF. Its job is to help you grow. But if you're serious about scale, your job is to eventually walk on your own.

Any Shame in it?

There's no shame in joining a GPO. In fact, there's more shame in ignoring one and bleeding margin to your better-organized competitors. But leadership means knowing when the velvet handshake becomes a velvet shackle.

Ask yourself: Is my GPO still driving my growth? Or am I feeding it? The answer may tell you more about your next five years than any rebate check will.

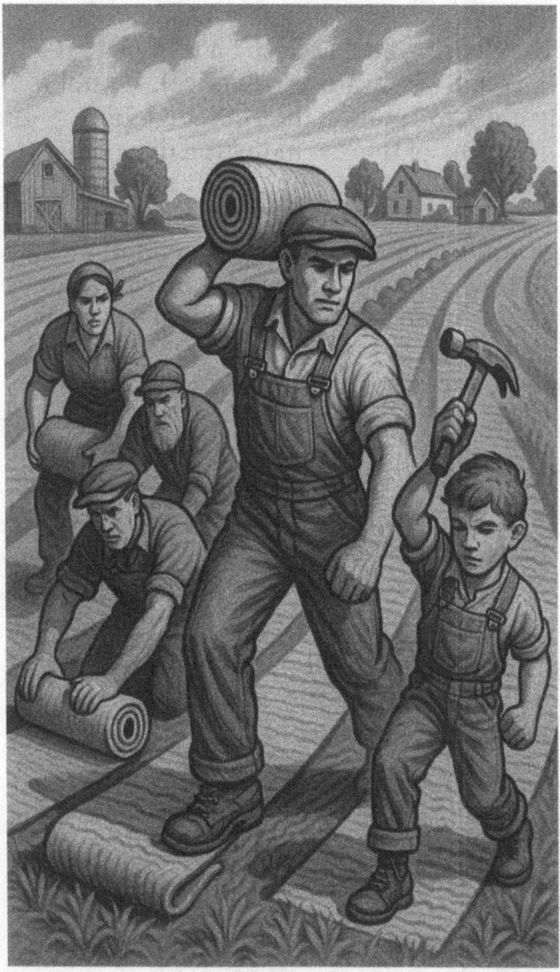

Chapter 19: The Gritty Bunch
The Tribe that Builds Us

The flooring business isn't a tech play. It's not SaaS (Software as a Service). It's not a frothy disruptor on the NASDAQ. It's a tribe, one of the last industrial diasporas built on craftsmanship, family networks, and blue-collar grit and the accessories a clever design and engineering cohort produce. This industry runs on relationships forged in job sites, not Zoom calls. It's a culture where loyalty is currency, where apprenticeship matters, and where respect is measured in how you show up and deliver. Not in likes or followers. Ignore that at your peril if you jump in the flooring pool. Because while flooring may look transactional on a spreadsheet, it is, and always will be, tribal at the core.

"A circle of trust is the most scalable structure in the world—because culture can accomplish what bureaucracy cannot."

Reed Hastings, LinkedIn Founder

At first glance, the flooring industry appears to be a realm of adhesives, substrates, square footage, SKU counts, and very few freak flags flying. I just put myself to sleep. A space dominated by logistics, craftsmanship, and commodity economics. But underneath all that, beneath the hardwood, the LVT, the polished concrete, lies something more enduring: a community tied not only by trade, but by temperament.

This is not a transient industry. It's a calling. It doesn't recruit; it absorbs. It rarely wavers from its traditional cultures or financial metrics. And those who stay are rarely here for the glamor. They are here for the grounding.

More than Muscle Memory

There is something psychologically particular about those drawn into flooring. This is an industry that requires high tolerance for friction, both literal and metaphorical. If you're intolerant to latency, run away. Installers, reps, owners, and specifiers all navigate uncertainty.

Much like oscillating trade policies. Shifting tastes, delayed shipments, botched measurements, and bad slabs are all on the menu. Interestingly, that fosters a deep shared emotional resilience.

I'm married to a psychologist. Don't ask. Her perspective on why people form tribes is pretty basic. Everyone wants to belong.

Belonging is a basic B level component at the base of Maslow's Hierarchy of Needs pyramid. Safety to express a view with others, without the fears inherent in human psychopathy. Shame. Exposure. Rejection. Failure. Public speaking, lol. That's a lot easier to navigate when you have a common understanding of a livelihood and the tradecraft that powers it. Flooring is such a place. There are about 330,000 of us that are conjoined because of its power to provide that sense of fearless belonging.

Our Industry is deeply populated with problem solvers, just not the kind who thrive in whiteboard brainstorms. We are doers. Tactile, spatial thinkers. People who feel a visceral satisfaction in the physicality of their work: leveling, measuring, fitting, smoothing.

These are the needs we desire as we've satisfied our basic B-level needs and begin to move further up the slopes of Maslow's pyramid toward self-actualization. Friendship. Respect. Recognition. Social Connection. Creativity. Fulfillment. This kinesthetic gratification of fulfilling a flooring project, the satisfaction of making a space whole and comforting draws in a certain psyche: the grounded realist with a streak of perfectionism.

There's also a quiet pride here. Flooring people rarely seek the spotlight. Well, maybe the burgeoning flooring podcast class, but I digress. You don't notice great flooring installation. You notice bad ones. This invisibility draws a personality type that finds dignity in essential work that's too often overlooked. Its blue-collar humility meets artisan exactitude.

We're Tribal, Not Local

Despite being hyperlocal, built initially on town-by-town relationships, the flooring industry is also a diaspora, a fragmented but interconnected society spread around the globe. Traveling reps, subcontract crews, trade show regulars, multi-generational business owners, and association memberships form a decentralized but emotionally cohesive tribe.

We use the same jargon: backorders, substrate moisture, mill direct, seam sealer, punch lists, plasticizer migration, coefficients of friction, ASTM standards, etc. And that language is often only understood inside the cohort. (BTW, learning the language of the trade should be among the first five slides in your onboarding deck.) This shared vernacular creates an "us" that survives even as business models shift from small-town family-owned shops to private equity rollups.

It's a space formed not by geography or ideology, but by the lived reality of tension. The friction between design and utility, price and quality, speed and craftsmanship.

Let's face it. Some of our species thrive on chaos management. It's plentiful in flooring and an essential element of our tribal nature.

Signal Through the Noise

EQ is the ability to read a room, bite your tongue, and get the project done with grace and aplomb. It's the ability to perceive, understand, use, and manage emotions in oneself and others. Emotional intelligence, especially in the form of relationship management and adaptability, is often the difference between survival and scale. It's a force multiplier. Flooring professionals must navigate architect vision, contractor chaos, feral installers, end-user expectations, and vendor performance. That's five balls in the air at the same time right there. Never seeing you sweat while you juggle is an EQ byproduct.

To survive this ecosystem, members develop:

1. Empathy: Reading a client's panic at a delayed shipment or misperceived color. Then calming it.

2. Patience: Waiting for a GC to give you a change order critical to the schedule.

3. Self-regulation: Enduring long cycles of deferred payment without erupting.

4. Social skill: Selling not just products, but peace of mind. That's an art form.

5. Business Decorum: Learn how to show up respectfully, well dressed, and with Knowledge sharing driven by manners.

Flooring pros are emotional tacticians, not just technical executors.

No Glamor, All Guts

Why does someone stay in an industry where rejection is common, margins are tight, products are unwieldy, every installation is bespoke with many mothers, and recognition is rare?

Because this community offers something many industries don't: a generational tether. Flooring is inherited, not often recruited. It's a father teaching his kid to measure a room and not forgetting all of its finish components. A daughter taking over the showroom. A rep with 30 years in a single territory who remembers every specifier by name.

The emotional continuity is powerful. And durable. A palpable example of entrepreneurship while gathered. And because unlike many knowledge industries, you can see the physical outcome of your work. You can walk on it. You can point to a building and say, "I did that." Check out design awards from NEOCON, Fuse, Starnet for the evidence. Beautiful examples of art, science, and dedication to a craft.

Those creations are statements of a time and place engineered and executed by craftsmen with aesthetic understanding and professional use of team. In a world increasingly disconnected, abstract, and virtual, that matters.

Surface Tension

The flooring community is not monolithic, but it is unified. Its connective tissue is temperament, tenacity, and trust. It's a culture and career that rewards grit over glamor, relationship over résumé, and finished work over fast talk. It's fostered thousands of millionaires. The explosive growth of sophisticated gangs like Fuse, Starnet, Diverzify, CCA, plus the accelerating presence of private equity in acquiring large chunks of it is proof that value is with us.

And maybe that's why it endures. While other industries busily chase speed and scale, the flooring community remains grounded. Literally and psychologically, in the act of preparing spaces for life to happen on top of it. That by its nature requires a technically adept process, seasoned with emotional quotient. A magnificent blending of art and science. Oftentimes a plodding technological and informed process grind, but also an artistic pursuit.

Yet, in flooring, those are the ties that bind us.

Conclusion: The Floor Is Yours

The flooring industry isn't for the faint of heart. It's not where easy money lives or where billionaires vacation. But it is where the people who build real tangible businesses, one relationship and one square foot at a time, create generational value. But only if they understand the battleground.

We've walked the corridors of indifference, survived the zero-sum price wars, and explored the strange quantum mechanics relative to the modern flooring business. We've seen how brand is not a logo, but a narrative. How margin is not an accounting term, but a mindset. How speed, adaptability, and technological adoption are no longer competitive advantages, they're prerequisites for survival.

This book isn't a playbook. It's a mirror. If you see yourself in these pages, whether as a leader, an aspirant, as an operator, or as someone who's spent years in the trenches of this trade, then you already know: the world isn't waiting for flooring, or you, to catch up.

Because in this business, the most important product you sell isn't carpet or hardwood. It's you.

Bibliography

Books

Ariely, Dan. *Predictably Irrational: The Hidden Forces That Shape Our Decisions*. New York: Harper Perennial, 2009.

Drucker, Peter F. *The Effective Executive: The Definitive Guide to Getting the Right Things Done*. New York: Harper Business, 2006.

Maslow, Abraham *Eupsychian Psychology*. Wiley Publishing, New Jersey, 1965. Republished as *Maslow on Management*. Wiley Publishing, New Jersey, 1998 by Ann R. Kaplan.

Ford, Martin. *Rule of the Robots: How Artificial Intelligence Will Transform Everything*. New York: Basic Books, 2021.

Galloway, Scott. *The Four: The Hidden DNA of Amazon, Apple, Facebook, and Google*. New York: Portfolio, 2017.

Gladwell, Malcolm. *Blink: The Power of Thinking Without Thinking*. New York: Little, Brown and Company, 2005.

Gladwell, Malcolm. *The Tipping Point: How Little Things Can Make a Big Difference*. New York: Little, Brown and Company, 2000.

Tsao, Frederick Chavalit. *Quantum Leadership: New Consciousness in

Business*. Singapore: World Scientific Publishing, 2022.

Tyson, Neil deGrasse. *Astrophysics for People in a Hurry*. New York: W. W. Norton & Company, 2017

Articles and Web Sources

"Blind Item Pricing and Margin Strategy." *Wood Floor Business*. Accessed May 2025. https://www.woodfloorbusiness.com.

"Quantum Physics Offers Insights About Leadership in the 21st Century." *Manage Magazine*. Accessed May 2025. https://managemagazine.com

"Quantum Leadership: Empowering SMEs in an AI-Driven Future." *Digital CXO*. Accessed May 2025. https://digitalcxo.com.

"23 Quotes on Failure from Super-Successful Leaders." *Entrepreneur*. Accessed May 2025. https://www.entrepreneur.com.

"Key Takeaways" *RSMUS* Accessed March 20, 2025, https://rsmus.com/insights/services/digital-transformation/ai-for-the-supply-chain.html

"Motivational Quotes for Entrepreneurs." *U.S. Chamber of Commerce CO*. Accessed May 2025. https://www.uschamber.com/co/start/strategy/motivational-quotes.

"Scott Galloway Tells Cannes Lions: 'The Era of Brand Is Over.'" *WARC*. Accessed May 2025. https://www.warc.com.

"Transom Capital completes acquisition of Galleher" https://www.galleher.com/newsworthy/transom-capital-completes-acquisition-of-galleher-expanding-into-the-premium-flooring-industry

"Pricing." *Wikipedia: The Free Encyclopedia*. Accessed May 2025. https://en.wikipedia.org/wiki/Pricing.

"Flooring Industry Statistics." *Get One Desk*. Accessed May 2025. https://www.getonedesk.com/flooring-industry-statistics.

"Psychological Pricing: Types, Advantages and Disadvantages." *Marketing91*. Accessed May 2025. https://www.marketing91.com/psychological-pricing/

"The power of reflection: An empirical examination of nostalgia advertising effects. Journal of Advertising, 33(3), 25–35".Muehling, D. D., & Sprott, D. E. (2004).

"Quantum Computing Principles." *Medium (by Park Windsor)*. Accessed May 2025. https://medium.com/@parkwindsor/quantum-computing-principles-fd00110b3a2e.

"Brand Positioning Concept." *iStock by Getty Images*. Accessed May 2025.

https://www.istockphoto.com/vector/brand-positioning-concept-vector-infographic-base-on-strategy-circle-diagram-has-gm1454145003-489881350.

"Flooring Market Expected to Reach USD 517.74 Billion by 2028 With a 5.4% CAGR." *Globe Newswire*. Accessed May 2025. https://www.globenewswire.com/news-release/2023/10/10/2757198/0/en/Flooring-Market-Expected-to-Reach-USD-517-74-Billion-by-2028-With-a-5-4-CAGR.html.

"Global Wood and Laminate Flooring Market." *Polaris Market Research*. Accessed May 2025. https://www.polarismarketresearch.com/industry-analysis/global-wood-and-laminate-flooring-market.

"Wood Laminate Flooring Market Report." *FactMR*. Accessed May 2025. https://www.factmr.com/report/482/wood-laminate-flooring-market.

"Vinyl Flooring Market Overview." *Book Clean Go*. Accessed May 2025. https://www.bookcleango.com/blog/flooring-industry-statistics.

"Vinyl Flooring Market Analysis." *Grand View Research*. Accessed May 2025. https://www.grandviewresearch.com/industry-analysis/vinyl-flooring-market.

"Global Flooring Market Size and Trends." *Business Wire*. Accessed May 2025.

https://www.businesswire.com/news/home/20211001005486/en/Global-Flooring-Market-Size-Share-Trends-Analysis-2021-2028.

"Laminate Flooring Market Forecast." *Consegic Business Intelligence*. Accessed May 2025. https://www.consegicbusinessintelligence.com/laminate-flooring-market.

"Flooring's Tough Year." *Floor Covering Weekly*. Accessed May 2025. https://www.floorcoveringweekly.com/main/features/floorings-tough-year-43386.

"Strong Start, Slow Finish." *Floor Covering Weekly*. Accessed May 2025. https://www.floorcoveringweekly.com/main/features/strong-start-slow-finish-41481.

"2023 Flooring Industry Year in Review." *Floor Trends Magazine*. Accessed May 2025. https://www.floortrendsmag.com/articles/111639-2023-flooring-industry-year-in-review.

Quotations from Public Figures

Bohr, Niels. "If you aren't confused by quantum mechanics, you haven't really understood it."

Churchill, Winston. "Success is not final; failure is not fatal: it is the courage to continue that counts."

Drucker, Peter F. "There is nothing so useless as doing efficiently that which should not be done at all."

Edison, Thomas. "Many of life's failures are people who did not realize how close they were to success when they gave up."

Heisenberg, Werner. "Uncertainty is not 'I don't know.' It is 'I can't know'.

Gates, Bill. "Success is a lousy teacher. It seduces smart people into thinking they can't lose.

Goff, Bob. "We are all rough drafts of the people we're still becoming.

Jobs, Steve. "I'm convinced that about half of what separates the successful entrepreneurs from the non-successful ones is pure perseverance."

Swingle, Brian. "Entanglement is the fabric of space-time."

Write Some Notes

www.ingramcontent.com/pod-product-compliance
Lightning Source LLC
Chambersburg PA
CBHW010329030426
42337CB00025B/4872